I0459033

Everton FC and St. Domingo's Church

HOW RELIGION TRANSFORMED FOOTBALL

BY

BOB WATERHOUSE

The moral rights of the author have been asserted.

All rights reserved.

No part of this publication maybe reproduced, stored in a retrieval system or transmitted in any form or by any means, without the prior permission in writing of the publisher, nor be otherwise circulated in any form of binding or cover other than that in which it is published and without a similar condition including this condition being imposed on the subsequent purchaser.

Paperback ISBN: 978-1-970463-04-0
Hardcover ISBN: 978-1-970463-05-7

DEDICATION

I would firstly like to dedicate this to my wife and two sons for their endless support in writing this book.

ACKNOWLEDGEMENT

My thanks must go to the staff of the Picton Library in Liverpool who assisted me in the research for this book. I would also like to thank retired academic Philp Garrahan for his endless help in editing, advising and inspiring the book.

TABLE OF CONTENTS

PREFACE

The nineteenth century was a time of incredible social, political and technological change.

The first Industrial Revolution of the eighteenth century was followed by a second, which not only exported industrialisation to other countries but also led to massive urbanisation. These developments led to significant potential problems for churches. In England, mainstream church attendance suffered in the new towns and cities while a whole host of new Christian groups emerged, such as Methodism, which started in the eighteenth century but developed in many of the industrial areas in the early nineteenth century. Other nonconformist churches were also expanding in these areas, as well as many spiritualist churches, which believed in contacting the dead.

The mainstream churches dealt with these issues in different ways. The Catholic church in 1870 at its First Vatican Council resorted to restating its traditional claim to be the preeminent church and to affirm the doctrine of papal infallibility, guaranteeing the pope's right to define Christian doctrine. Meanwhile, the Church of England was becoming increasingly divided. On one side stood the High Church Oxford Movement, led by John Henry Newman, which sought to restore traditional Catholic faith and practices within Anglicanism. On the other hand was the Low Church movement, which promoted a more Evangelical approach, focusing on spreading the church's influence in newly industrialised areas, an approach aligned with the efforts of Methodists and other Protestant denominations.

From this movement sprang the new doctrine of muscular Christianity, which sought to spread the word of God by encouraging active physical activity. At the same time, the working week was gradually being reduced to give the working class more leisure time. Initially, this only affected women and children when the Factories Act 1847 limited their hours to a 58-hour week in the textiles industry, subsequently extended to all factories in 1867.[1]

By 1875, working hours for males were also reduced in most industries to between 50 and 56 hours, which often included a half-day on Saturdays. These were the conditions that allowed the spread of Association football from the upper middle classes in the mid-nineteenth century through the mainstream middle class and, finally, in the last few decades of the century, to the working class.

In the Everton area of Liverpool, one of the major social changes in the nineteenth century was the gradual replacement of its traditional population of wealthy merchants with both the middle class and the working class, the latter of which became clustered in terraced streets, many of which became slums in the twentieth century.

One of the district's institutions to experience these changes was the Anglican St. George's Church. It was opened in 1814 for the benefit of the relatively affluent local population. However, by the late nineteenth century, many of these residents had moved on, and the church experienced serious financial problems, including being unable to afford the stipend of the minister. Consequently, control of the church fell to the Ecclesiastical Commissioners of England. [2] Into this void emerged a number of Nonconformist churches.

In the early years of the century, the Congregationalist Crescent Chapel opened in the district and at the end, under Reverend Robert Veitch, the church reached out into the community with new styles of service such as 'open' worship on Sundays and free Sunday morning breakfasts combined with the setting up of youth organisations.[3]

Methodism grew rapidly in nineteenth-century Liverpool, expanding from five churches in 1800 to forty in 1900. A particular feature of Methodism in Liverpool under the leadership of the Reverend Charles Garrett was its attachment to teetotalism. [4] This was to have a particular effect on the development of Everton Football Club, which originated from the football club set up by St. Domingo's New Connexion Methodist Church in 1878.

INTRODUCTION

Everton and Liverpool aren't the only top-flight football clubs whose early origins owe a debt to Christianity. Peter Lupson, in his excellent book on the subject in 2006, linked no less than nearly a third of clubs, which had then played in the Premier League, to a church.[1] In his book, he documents twelve clubs that were set up by various churches and Sunday schools in the late nineteenth century. Football writer Haider Jawad estimates that between thirty and thirty-five of the current Premier League and Football League clubs were originally founded by churches. Additionally, he notes that public expressions of religious faith by players have become relatively commonplace in recent years, whereas such displays were comparatively rare during the 1980s and 1990s.[2]

This book aims to understand the beliefs that underpinned the movement for the church to influence sport in the late Victorian period. It investigates how the Church played a pivotal role in the formation of many of today's major league football clubs.

It also examines the role of religion in the global spread of football and its ongoing influence on the game. While particular attention is given to the impact of Christianity, the book also considers more recent examples of how other faiths, such as Islam and Judaism, have shaped the sport. It traces how the Church gradually withdrew from its earlier involvement in football, yet highlights substantial evidence that religion continues to play a significant role in the game today, with new clubs even continuing to be founded on religious principles.

The book concludes by assessing the evidence that the Methodist church St. Domingo's was the key founding influence on Everton FC, as documented in Lupson's book and many other historical accounts. Moreover, it also addresses revisionist perspectives that question St. Domingo's central role, particularly in light of the fact that, by 1885, 25 of the 112 football clubs in Liverpool had religious affiliations. Sports historian James Walvin, for instance, identifies four churches in Liverpool as having played a crucial part in the early development of football clubs.[3]

In its final chapter, the book assesses whether it was the New Connection Methodist Church of St Domingo's or the Anglican Everton United Church that played the decisive role in the formation of Everton FC.

CHAPTER 1

MUSCULAR CHRISTIANITY

I will argue that the mid-nineteenth-century movement in British Protestant churches called muscular Christianity had a pivotal influence on the formation of many early English football clubs, notably Everton and Liverpool. I will also argue that in Scotland, muscular Catholicism had a similar influence on the formation of several catholic clubs, most notably Glasgow Celtic.

C. Putney defines muscular Christianity as '*a Christian commitment to health and manliness.*'[1]

Donald E. Hall has a slightly more detailed description:

'*An association between physical strength, religious certainty, and the ability to control the world around oneself.*'[2]

There are several New Testament references to the virtues of maintaining physical health, notably 1 *Corinthians 6:9-20 on physical health and Mark 11:15* on manly exertion. However, since the founding of the church by St. Paul, the Christian ethos was dominated by the seeking of spiritual salvation. In the words of St. Paul – '*godliness profits a man much more than bodily exercise.*'[3]

Unlike the Ancient Greeks and Romans, who venerated physical sports like the Olympic Games, early Christianity was suspicious of sports as influencing man to turn away from spiritual salvation. They were influenced by an Augustinian view of the world, which saw the body and soul being separated, with the danger that the body could transcend the

1

superior form of the soul. So early ascetic Christians tried to mortify the body by starving it, whipping it, or depriving it of sleep. [4] Later Christians, such as the Puritans, were concerned that sports such as early football were associated with gambling and violence. In 1531, the Puritan preacher Thomas Eliot argued that *'football caused beastly fury and extreme violence,'* and in 1572, the Bishop of Rochester demanded a new campaign to suppress *'this evil game'.* [5]

The emphasis on spiritual rather than physical salvation persisted well into the nineteenth century. It was during this time that the newly established Methodist Church, other Nonconformist groups, and the emerging class of urban professionals began to engage with sport—initially by using their influence in Parliament to outlaw traditional medieval pastimes such as cockfighting and bearbaiting, notably through the passing of the Prevention of Cruelty to Animals Act in 1835.

This alliance of forces also started to restrict the traditional playing of mob football through measures such as the 1835 Highways Act, which banned street football in urban areas. At the same time, traditional Shrovetide games of football in Middlesex and Surrey were also closed. The large and violent mass football game in Ashbourne, Derbyshire, which still survives today, was controlled by the army and the reading out of the Riot Act. [6]

After the Chartist protests of the late 1830s and 1840s, politicians began to consider strategies to reduce future protests by adopting a more positive relationship with sport. Robert Slaney, a politician then in office, suggested that the *neglected classes* were in dire need of *regulated amusement,* which would act as a *safety valve for their eager energies.*[7]

There were also worries within the military, after the Crimean War, about the fitness of their recruits. This led to the introduction of athletics in military training, which had an interesting by-product, fraternisation within ranks. Eventually, organised games like cricket and rugby were developed within the ranks.[8]

But the main background factor behind muscular Christianity was the general nineteenth-century crisis in religion. This was creating fears of a growing secularisation in the cities where the working class were increasingly not going to church. The Industrial Revolution gave rise to rapidly expanding cities in which the Church found itself increasingly out of touch with the growing urban population.

The population of these cities grew dramatically in the early nineteenth century as large sections of the population moved from the countryside to the burgeoning cities. In 1800, only 20 per cent of the British population lived in cities; by 1850, it was 50 per cent.[9] Although London continued to grow at this time, its share of the urban population fell. This was due to the large urban clusters emerging around cities like Manchester, Liverpool and Birmingham. The growth of the former two was particularly stark; in 1700, both had no more than 2500 inhabitants, and by 1851, both had over 300,000.

Manchester and Birmingham's growth was fueled by the presence of nearby coal, while another factor, particularly in Liverpool's case, was the growth of market access caused by the development of transport infrastructure and technology. [10]

The consequences for Britain's traditional churches appeared to be devastating as the new industrial working class didn't seem to be going to church. The 1851 Religious Census showed that fewer than half the adult population went to church on Sundays. The highest rates of abstention were for the working class in the newly industrialised areas.[11]

The historian Owen Chadwick believes that this was because of

– the inability of the churches' machine to adapt itself quickly enough to new areas, new suburbs, new towns…… the consequence of the collapse of the parochial system.[12]

The historian Hugh McLeod saw an anticlericalism flourishing, which led to the creation of new religions and a decline of attendance at the Church of England.[13] Among the new religions formed was a whole plethora of new Protestant religions, which were all characterised by a more literal reading of the Bible. These included Pentecostalism, Seventh Day Adventists, Mormonism, Jehovah's Witnesses and Christian Science.[14] All of these religions challenged the mainstream churches, which were already threatened by the rise of Methodism and Nonconformist churches.

Another historian, Callum G Brown, identified a dominant evangelical religion in these mainstream nineteenth-century English churches, which idealised women as examples of moral goodness and viewed men as immoral and needing to be guided by pious, loving and caring women.[15] This form of religion was increasingly considered to be driving men away from the church.

The Anglo-American Protestant churches viewed this as a 'Crisis in masculinity'. It was particularly directed, initially, at the Upper and Middle classes. The background to the 'crisis' was the profound set of changes to the workforce triggered by the industrial revolution. From an American perspective, Brett and Kate McKay have described this situation as:

4

'Men were moving from the field to the factory and also getting jobs in the emerging white-collar sector. Earning a living required less sweat of the brow, and more repetitive lever pulling and sedentary mind work. Living in crowded, artificially engineered cities meant men no longer had to pit themselves against nature's unpredictable elements.' [16]

Gradually, these concerns were taken on by the Protestant churches. There was a growing recognition that the congregations and ethos of the church were becoming increasingly feminised. In America, the McKays noted that –

church memberships in the late 19th century skewed up to ¾ female, and services were described as a "kind of weekly Mother's Day" — meetings filled with praises to womanhood, sweet sermons, and sentimental music. The ministers and few men who did attend seemed to observers to be even less healthy and more effeminate than the general population. [17]

It must also be said that muscular Christianity was by no means exclusively Protestant. Rebecca Alpert has identified a specific type of muscular Catholicism which incorporated a more communitarian approach, such as partaking in the sacrament as a means of achieving athletic success.

In the USA, the Catholic church promoted athletic programmes at leading schools and universities such as Notre Dame in Indiana. These included the American football team at Notre Dame's South Bend, the athletic leagues at the Roman Catholic High School in Philadelphia and the athletic leagues of the Catholic Youth Organization in Chicago. [18]

The term 'muscular Christianity' first starts being used as a reaction to some of the English mid-nineteenth-century novels like Charles Kingsley's 1857 novel *Two Years Ago* and Thomas Hughes' international 1856 best-seller *Tom Brown's Schooldays*. The term itself was first used explicitly by the critic

T.S. Sanders in reviewing *Two Years Ago* and was then widely used to refer to *Tom Brown's Schooldays*. [19] The books embodied the fears that the Anglican church was becoming too feminine and that young men needed to combine the traditional Christian ethics of gentlemanly behaviour with masculine camaraderie and athleticism.[20]

In Kingsley's novel *Westward Ho!* He attacked the Catholic church, in particular, its asceticism and condemnation of the flesh, which were feminising Victorian culture. [21]

By contrast, Kingsley and Hughes venerated physical activity as this quote from Thomas Hughes illustrates – *God intends us to enjoy all his good gifts, including the physical pleasures of cricket and football, swimming and running, hunting and fishing – and indeed the sexual relationship between man and wife.*[22]

Sport would provide the perfect vehicle for future gentlemen to enter the world of work with a healthy and moral spirit of competition, as this quote from Charles Kingsley encapsulates:

Through sport boys acquire virtues which no books can give them: not merely daring and endurance, but better still, temper, self-restraint, fairness, honour, unenvious appropriation of another's success and all that 'give and take' of life which stand a man in good stead when he goes forth into the world and without which, indeed, his success is always maimed and partial. [23]

The historian Norman Vance prefers the term 'Christian manliness' to Muscular Christianity. He sees the movement as a reaction against the other-worldly views of neo-catholic and evangelical nonconformist groups, which were failing to engage with the social deprivation and class division of the mid-nineteenth century. The new philosophy put the emphasis on social action and was influenced by the Christian Socialist movement, which, in reaction to the violence of the Chartist movement in the 1830s, saw tackling social deprivation and class division as essential to the nation's survival.[24] Charles Kingsley and Thomas Hughes were proponents of Christian Socialism.

The movement disseminated its ideas through two Journals, *Politics of the People* and *The Christian Socialist*. In 1854, F.D. Maurice founded the Working Men's College in London 1854 to educate the masses. Under the influence of Maurice, theological circles shifted their emphasis from Atonement to Incarnation, which effectively shifted Christian thinking to creating an embodied soul through athleticism and physical strength in the formation of character.[25]

These ideas were gradually exported to America in the late nineteenth century and began to influence politicians such as Theodore Roosevelt, who was concerned that the social trends already examined, combined with non-Protestant immigration, posed a threat to the traditionally privileged social standing of White Anglo-Saxon Protestant males. The pioneer psychologist G. Stanley Hall also pointed to the attempts of muscular Christianity to make American Protestant churches more masculine:

'…women's influence in church had led to an overabundance of sentimental hymns, effeminate clergymen and sickly-sweet images of Jesus. These things were repellent to "real men" and boys, averred critics, who argued that males would avoid church until "feminized" Protestantism gave way to muscular Christianity, a strenuous religion for the strenuous life.' [26]

Arguably, the philosophy was already being enacted through the style of teaching encouraged by Thomas Arnold at Rugby School since 1828, when he was appointed headmaster. He believed that sport was a good method for encouraging responsibility and that football was a vehicle for the character building of young men who would be future leaders.[27] An alternative explanation from the sports historian David Goldblatt was that the teaching of formal sport was a way for the staff to take control of previously unruly students whose games were chaotic and unregulated. For example, the Eton Field Game was banned from 1827 to 1836 because of the fears of violence and unruliness among the boys. In any case, sport flourished on the playing fields of late nineteenth-century British Public schools. This is amply illustrated by the expansion of those fields at that time. In 1845, Harrow had only eight acres of sports fields; by 1900, it had expanded to 146. Charterhouse moved out of its cramped facilities for the open fields and land of Surrey.

Historian J.A. Mangan observed that one striking difference between images of Marlborough College in 1834 and those from 1851 is the presence of playing fields adjacent to the school. This was a direct result of the school priest, G.E.L. Cotton, creating games fields and splitting the boys into competitive houses as a deliberate policy to regulate the previous disruptive behaviour of the boys and create what he called 'Christian manliness'. Mangan sees these values as later being exported to the colonies to create a universal 'brave, truthful and Christian gentleman'.[28] This will be explored further in Chapter 3.

Also, in the 1840s and 1850s, the leading universities were provided with magnificent sporting facilities. In these environments, the sport of football particularly flourished.[29]

From the mid-nineteenth century, the churches also began to explore connections with sport. The philosophy of muscular Christianity, which so many of the trainee vicars were learning at the time, made them particularly keen to promote their beliefs in the community. Donald E Hall saw these beliefs as:

'…combining physical strength, religious certainty, and the ability to shape and control the world around oneself'. [30]

Early muscular Christians saw sports as a way of evangelising the unchurched, especially the highly masculine tough guys who were increasingly absent from church. An 1894 article about the Reverend AO Jay on his work in the East End of London reported that this High Church clergyman *discovered that the boxing-gloves are most useful, though neglected weapons in the armory of the church.* Boxing led to Jay finding many of these men coming to his church pews, and of them being less prone to violence subsequently. [31]

The Anglican Church was particularly eager to move away from 'puritanism,' which was seen as having alienated ordinary people. This was especially true in relation to sport, which began to grow significantly from the mid-nineteenth century onwards. [32]

In Birmingham, for example, the total number of football clubs had grown from one in 1874 to 155 in 1880. In the same city from 1871 to 1880, twenty per cent of the cricket teams and twenty-five per cent of the football clubs had connections with religious organisations. [33]

The Christian emphasis on athleticism was also promoted by the YMCA, which was founded in London in 1844 by George Williams, who was concerned about the lack of healthy activities for young men in the cities, with their only options being taverns or brothels.[34]

'Initially the strongly evangelical YMCA would have paid little attention to the Anglican ideas of Hughes and Kingsley but attitudes started to change in the 1850's after two addresses to the YMCA by the Anglican William Beal and the Baptist Hugh Stowell Brown extolling the benefits of physical exercise.'[35]

In America, the YMCA's emphasis on meetings in gyms led to the invention of volleyball and basketball. Both sports were developed by the headmaster of Springfield College, Luther H. Gullick Jr. He was a devotee of muscular Christianity who institutionalised it within the YMCA. He believed that both sports favoured the principles of loyalty, self-control, self-sacrifice and teamwork, which he considered to be the foundations of Christianity and an altruistic Christian.

Basketball was invented by James Naismith, a young sports teacher under Gullick, who was given the task of tackling the behaviour of naughty schoolboys. It was later disseminated by the wider YMCA movement.[36] The latter also encouraged churches to organise camping and public playground movements.[37]

In England, the YMCA also played an active role in promoting working-class sport. For example, in 1894, an Anglican vicar, Arthur Osborne Montgomery, built a gymnasium with a boxing ring in the basement of Holy Trinity church in Shoreditch, where he organised popular boxing tournaments. In 1882, members of the Burnley YMCA turned to football.[38]

In South America, the YMCA became the organisation which spread the variant of indoor 5-a-side football known as

Futsal throughout the continent. The sport was originally invented in Montevideo in 1930 by Juan Carlos Ceriani for use inside YMCAs. In Brazil, which is now the heartland of Futsal, the rules were modified.[39]

There is also much evidence that muscular Christianity was a strong influence on Baron de Coubertin, who founded the modern Olympic Games in 1896. He visited England and became a fan of Thomas Arnold whilst visiting Rugby School. De Coubertin was another Catholic pioneer of muscular Christianity.[40]

Muscular Christianity was essentially a new strategy to combat both the perceived feminisation of mainstream churches and the challenge of new religions during the early Industrial Revolution. One of the unintended consequences of this new philosophy was to influence many churches to set up football clubs in late nineteenth-century England and Scotland. This will be further examined in the next chapter.

CHAPTER 2

THE CHURCH AND FOOTBALL IN THE UK

Churches in the mid-nineteenth century were facing a crisis in working-class participation. In the 1880s, H. McLeod estimated that 15–20% of the London working class attended church, compared with 40% of the middle class. The figures for Bristol were 40% and 60% respectively.[1] There was a particular problem for the Anglican Church in the north of England, where the population was increasing most rapidly due to industrialisation. This is illustrated by the experiences of E. R. Wickham, an Anglican priest in Sheffield at the time, who records that in the first half of the nineteenth century, there was conclusive evidence of the urban working class's reluctance to attend church. Even in the late nineteenth century—often seen as a golden age of religion—he found that the religious revival was largely confined to the upper and middle classes.[2]

However, Nonconformist churches, such as the Methodists, Presbyterians and Baptists, were rapidly rising, particularly in the 1830s and 1840s. So successful were they that by the time of the first church attendance census in 1851, Nonconformist church attendance made up almost half of the total and was higher than that of the Anglican Church in the larger manufacturing areas.[3] The Methodist Church, founded by John Wesley, was rooted in the principle of spreading the gospel to the working classes. It was also renowned for its charitable work supporting the sick and poor—something which held particular appeal in the industrial cities.[4]

The attraction of Nonconformist churches to the working class is evident in A. D. Gilbert's analysis of Nonconformist burial records from 1800–1837, which suggested that artisans formed the largest group; together with labourers and miners, they constituted three-quarters of the total.[5] At the same time, millenarian movements such as the Jehovah's Witnesses and Pentecostalism were gaining traction among the working class. Their belief in the sudden transformation of society often provided comfort to those struggling to come to terms with the profound social changes wrought by the Industrial Revolution.[6]

The decline in working-class Anglican attendance, the comparative success of Nonconformist churches in inner cities, and the rise of muscular Christianity all influenced the Church's involvement in late nineteenth-century football.

Despite the long tradition of street football—characterised by mass participation and dating back to the Middle Ages—the development of codified football in the nineteenth century was led by elite public schools. Each school developed its own distinctive version of the game, eventually contributing to the standardisation of rules later in the century. For example, at Winchester College, the game was played in 1825 with 25 players per side, using lines scored in the earth as goals set 27 yards apart. Dribbling was banned, and the main objective was to charge down the opponents' shots.[7]

Football was valued at these schools as a critical component in preparing future leaders of the British Empire. It was also seen as an antidote to the perceived moral dangers threatening public schoolboys, such as masturbation, effeminacy, and homosexuality. Many schools—such as Rugby—were located in regions with a long football tradition.

In Rugby, for instance, football had been played on New Year's Day since the early 1700s. This heritage, combined with Matthew Arnold's advocacy of muscular Christianity, laid fertile ground for the development of public-school football. Rugby's version received particular endorsement in 1864 when the Clarendon Commission's report on the state of English public schools singled it out for praise.[8]

Between the publication of *Tom Brown's Schooldays* in 1857 and the formation of the Football Association (FA) in 1863, numerous football clubs were established by privately educated young men. Some of these, such as the Wanderers and the Royal Engineers, would go on to play key roles in the development of the game.[9]

A major impetus for a common set of rules came from Cambridge University, which sought to enable boys from different public schools to play together. As a result, a meeting in 1848 led to Eton, Winchester, Harrow, Rugby, and Shrewsbury adopting uniform rules so that students arriving at Cambridge all played by the same standards.[10] This meeting is commemorated today by a monument on the corner of Parker's Piece in Cambridge, at the site where the original rules were pinned to a tree.[11]

The Cambridge initiative eventually led, in 1863, to a meeting in London where representatives of leading football clubs—many of whom were former public schoolboys—came together to establish a unified code of rules and form the Football Association. Armed with these rules, public school alumni ventured into industrial cities to promote football as a means of improving the health and morals of the working class.[12]

However, not everyone agreed on the rules. Blackheath, which preferred the hacking style of play popular at Rugby School, resigned from the FA and, eight years later, became one of the founding members of the Rugby Football Union. [13] Nonetheless, the dominant voices opposed hacking. As Ebenezer Morley, the FA's secretary, famously stated:

If we have hacking, no one who has arrived at the age of discretion will play at football and it will be entirely left to schoolboys.[14]

Handling was not fully eliminated from the Association game until the London-based FA amalgamated with the much larger Sheffield FA. This union led to handling-based clubs breaking away and forming the Rugby Football Union in 1871. [15]

Why, then, did the Sheffield FA develop so early in the history of the game? According to Tony Collins, the local economy—based on small-scale, highly skilled metal manufacturing—meant that the working class had both the time and disposable income to engage in or spectate early football matches. Sheffield had also been a cricket stronghold since the 1820s, and many cricketers played football in the off-season, fostering a vibrant local sporting culture. Nottingham shared similar traits, and it is no coincidence that both cities became home to some of the world's earliest football clubs. [16]

The fact that Sheffield FA was larger than the London-based Football Association has prompted some revisionist theories that downplay the role of public schools in football's rise. One example is Turton Football Club in Lancashire. It had been assumed that the club was founded in 1871 by two former public schoolboys, J. C. and Robert Kay. However, P. Swain has shown that by that time the club already had 48 members, each paying a one-shilling subscription. He also argues that the shared cultural identity of the cotton towns facilitated the game's spread more rapidly than in the more diverse cities of Liverpool and Manchester.[17]

Yet the founding members of Sheffield Cricket Club—who, in 1857, decided to play football during the winter—were privately educated men who viewed the club as an elite institution. They even wrote to public schools requesting copies of their football rulebooks. Football historian Tony Collins has documented several examples of how the Sheffield FA adopted rules from public school games, including the allowance of a *rouge*—an Eton rule permitting players to score if they touched down the ball after it passed between the *rouge* flags.[18]

There is also evidence to suggest that Harrow School played a significant role in influencing the origins of future football clubs in its northern heartland. In 1870, as already mentioned, two Harrovian brothers, John and Robert Kay, were instrumental in creating Turton FC in an isolated village between Blackburn and Bolton. Soon afterwards, three Old Harrovian sons of mill owner Nathaniel Walsh established Darwen FC, whose players were employed at their father's mill. The club became an early pioneer of professional football and broke into the public-school exclusivity of the FA Cup by becoming the first northern club to reach the quarter-finals in 1879.[19] Revisionists seeking to downplay the role of public schools in developing football appear to have overstated their case.

This book accepts that in many areas there were pre-existing football clubs that supported the development of the game, but argues that the primary vehicle for spreading football was the Church. This influence began with religious figures holding key positions in the FA, such as Lord Kinnaird, who served as FA President from 1890 to 1923 and was also the Lord High Commissioner of the Church of Scotland.[20] Later, it stemmed from clergy embedded in local communities. At the time, theology was a core university subject, and young men training for the priesthood were deeply influenced by muscular Christianity and a desire to improve working-class male morality. As the social historian James Walvin remarked in his pioneering 1975 work:

'Among many of the younger curates, the belief in athleticism was almost as striking as their belief in God. Few doubted the need for large-scale recreation as part of the Churches' solution to the 'Condition of England Question'. Clergymen seized on football as the ideal way of combating urban degeneracy and, as a result, working-class churches began to spawn football teams in the years immediately following the concession of free Saturday afternoons in local industries.' [21]

By the mid to late nineteenth century, the Church of England was actively training clergy for ministry in industrial regions. This was part of a wider expansion that saw its clergy nearly double in number from 14,613 in 1841 to 24,232 in 1891. The Additional Curates Society also funded more curates in inner-city parishes.[22]

Initially, Anglican clergy favoured cricket. One of the earliest books celebrating it as England's *national game* was written by the Devon vicar, Rev. James Pycroft, who declared: *The game of cricket, philosophically considered, is a standing panegyric to the English character.* [23] It is perhaps no coincidence that many future football clubs founded by churches began as church cricket teams. Aston Villa is a notable example. The club's name was inspired by the mansion opposite the Wesleyan chapel that established the club. In 1872, some members of the

Young Men's Bible Class formed a cricket team called *The Aston Villa (Wesleyan) Cricket Club*. The club's formation was significantly aided by the church minister, 51-year-old Frederick Briggs, who was the circuit superintendent and whose permission would have been necessary.

By chance, two years later, four of its members witnessed a football match being played on local waste ground. Wanting to stay fit in winter, they decided to form a football team. However, the match they saw was played under Rugby rules, which they deemed too dangerous. Consequently, they chose to adopt the Association Football rules agreed in 1863. [24] Several other Birmingham cricket teams also formed football clubs. These included Aston Unity, which disbanded in 1908 as players kept leaving for Aston Villa, and Walsall Town FC, which later became Walsall Swifts and eventually Walsall FC.[25]

The cricketing influence was crucial in the founding of what is arguably the world's first football club, Sheffield FC, established in 1857. Though not formed by a church, it was started by local businessmen who were members of Sheffield Cricket Club and wanted to keep fit in the winter. This was also true of Notts County FC, the world's oldest professional football club, founded in 1862 and shaped by the city's strong cricketing culture.[26]

However, the world's first church football team was also established in Sheffield. It was set up in 1861 by Cemetery Road Congregational Church, and a commemorative plaque was unveiled on the original site in May 2024. Sheffield is also home to the oldest church to have formed a football club: Heeley Christ Church FC, established in 1862.[27]

There is a long list of current professional football clubs in England that were originally founded by churches. In addition to the twelve listed by Peter Lupson, in 1877, boys from St Luke's Church in Blakenhall founded a team that would become Wolverhampton Wanderers. Blackpool also originated from the local St John's Church. [28] Much later, Arsenal FC relocated to its North London ground in Highbury, which was leased from St John's College of Divinity. The lease prohibited the sale of intoxicating liquor on matchdays and barred matches on holy days. These restrictions were lifted in 1925 when the club purchased the ground.[29]

Another club with religious origins is Exeter City. It began in 1901 as St Sidwell's United, composed of players from Exeter Wesleyan United. The team likely had links to the Wesleyan Chapel and Sunday School on Sidwell Street and included many boys from St Sidwell's School. The name was changed to Exeter City in 1904.[30]

Lupson first mentions Bolton Wanderers, founded in 1874 by pupils and teachers at Christ Church in Bolton. They became known as Bolton Wanderers in 1877. One of the key figures was the vicar of Christ Church, Joseph Farrall Wright, who, although not a sportsman, was a keen advocate of muscular Christianity. He believed that sports such as football and cricket cultivated character traits like courage, self-control, fair play and unselfishness. He passed these beliefs on to Christ Church School's headmaster, Tom Ogden, a football enthusiast who had played the game at college. Ogden chose to follow the Football Association rules used by Turton FC, making the club the second in Lancashire to play Association football. The name 'Wanderers' was adopted in 1877 after the club had to find a new ground due to a split with Christ Church.[31]

The club made history on 8 September 1888, when Kenny Davenport scored the first ever goal in the Football League. This fact was only confirmed in 2013 when football historians Marc Metcalf and Robert Botling discovered that the Aston Villa versus Wolverhampton Wanderers match had been delayed, thereby ruling out the previously accepted own goal by Villa's Gershom Cox.[32]

The direct influence of Rugby School is evident in the formation of Barnsley Football Club by Reverend Tiverton Preedy. He trained at Lincoln Theological College, whose founder, Edward Benson, had been an assistant master at Rugby School from 1852 to 1858. The book *Tom Brown's Schooldays* was published during Benson's time there, and its values of muscular Christianity were central to Preedy's training. As vicar of St Peter's Church in Barnsley, he founded a sports club that played by Association Football rules, having fallen out with Barnsley Rugby Club for holding a match on Good Friday. The team was originally known as Barnsley St Peter's FC. After Preedy's departure, it dropped the 'St Peter's' and became Barnsley FC in 1897. The following year, it joined the Second Division.[33]

According to Peter Lupson, muscular Christianity was a guiding force behind the early formation of Manchester City. This influence came through Anna Connell, the eldest daughter of Reverend Arthur Connell, rector of St Mark's Church in West Gorton. Shocked by the poor conditions in the newly incorporated town, she was inspired by her sister's efforts with mothers' meetings at the church. Anna began weekly meetings for men, offering talks, music, drama and recitals. One of her co-organisers, William Beastow, a linesman at St Mark's, formed a cricket team in 1879 and a football team the following year. Thus, St Mark's Football Club was born. It became Gorton AFC, then Ardwick AFC, and finally, in 1894, Manchester City. Ardwick had already been admitted to the Football League's Second Division in 1891, and the new team simply took its place.[34]

However, subsequent research by Andrew Keenan has challenged Lupson's view that West Gorton was facing significant social problems at the time of the club's formation. Keenan claims the area was virtually crime-free and that the football team mainly recruited middle-class boys. Its first captain, William Sumner, was a university student, and the squad included the son and stepson of William Beastow, who managed the Union Ironworks. Keenan found that the team was formed not in response to crime or poverty, but due to concerns about the declining number of young men attending church. These concerns had been publicly raised by Bishop Fraser of Manchester in the same year. Arthur Connell was also reportedly eager to gain favour with the bishop, having been requesting a curate for some time.[35] Despite their differences, both researchers agree on the strong influence of muscular Christianity in the club's formation. It is notable that early football clubs mainly recruited from the middle class and skilled working class, as the broader working class lacked both the leisure time and the habit of attending church.

Manchester United, unlike its city rival, was not founded by a church. It was established in 1878 by railway workers from the Newton Heath carriage and wagon department of the Lancashire and Yorkshire Railway. In its early years, the team was composed entirely of Protestants, as Catholics were barred from employment at the city's ironworks at the time.[36] Nevertheless, the club developed a long-standing association with the Catholic community. One of its original fans, Louis Rocca—son of Italian Catholic immigrants—later became the club's assistant manager. In 1902, he proposed the name Manchester Celtic, which was rejected in favour of Manchester United. As Chief Scout in the 1930s, Rocca used his ties to the Manchester Catholic Sportsman's Club to build a scouting network through the Catholic Church. This effort unearthed players such as Johnny Carey and Stan Pearson. Another member of the Catholic Sportsman's Club was Manchester City's wing half Matt Busby. In 1945, Rocca played a key role in appointing Busby as Manchester United's manager. Busby was one of several Catholic managers who led the club until the 1980s.[37]

Birmingham was a particularly fertile area for church influence on sport, as in the 1880s, over a quarter of all football and cricket clubs had their roots in the church.[38] Like many church-founded football clubs in the late nineteenth century, Birmingham City began as a cricket club. It was established in 1871 at Holy Trinity Church in Bordesley. By 1875, members of the club wished to maintain their fitness during the winter months. Six members of the team decided to form a football club, which they named *Small Heath Alliance*. The group was led by William Henry Edmonds, an accountant who was to be married at Holy Trinity in 1876. He became the club's first secretary and captain. His background was notably middle-class. In 1879, the club faced the already established Aston Villa for the first time. In 1888, they became the first club in the country to form a limited liability company with a board of directors and dropped the word *Alliance* from their title. They eventually adopted the name *Birmingham City* in 1905.[39] As with many early successful clubs, they benefitted from the involvement of local businessmen from an early stage. Their first captain, Billy Edmunds, was a prosperous local businessman, and Harry Morris, a former player credited with securing the St Andrew's ground in 1906, also became a businessman and club director.[40] The speed with which the club distanced itself from Holy Trinity exemplifies the trajectory of nearly all church-based clubs.[41] This has led some historians, such as Richard Holt, to argue that these early sporting initiatives originated more from ordinary church members than from the clergy.[42]

The club adopted professionalism in 1885, and in 1892 they were invited to play in the Second Division of the Football League. They were initially very successful, becoming champions in their first season, although they lost the test match for promotion. The following season, they again won the league and, this time, successfully defeated Darwen to reach the First Division.[43]

In 1879, a vicar and churchwarden at St Andrew's Church in Fulham founded what became the oldest football club in London. Seeking to create a youth club with a sporting focus, the Reverend Cardwell approached the 15-year-old Tom Norman after observing him and his friends playing cricket and football informally. Like many early football clubs, the initial reports in the parish magazine referred only to the cricket team. It was not until 1883 that the club secured a football pitch at the Ranelagh Club, near the Putney Bridge railway arch. In 1886, its name changed to *Fulham St Andrew's Cricket and Football Club*, due to the existence of several other St Andrew's football clubs in West London. In 1894, the club moved to its current home at Craven Cottage. A cottage belonging to Lord Craven had stood on the site since 1780, but after a fire destroyed it in 1888, the land became overgrown. Because the site lay beside the River Thames and was six feet below river level, it was not until 1896 that the ground was sufficiently developed to host its first football match. When the club became a limited liability company in 1903, the name *St Andrew's* was dropped from the title. However, the church still stands and features a commemorative plaque marking the club's origins. In 1907, the club was admitted to the Second Division of the Football League, following two years of topping the Southern League. [44]

Unlike early architectural icons such as Aston Villa's Trinity Road stand, Fulham's Craven Cottage grandstand holds listed building status and will remain protected. The land itself can claim a rich footballing and historical legacy. It once formed part of the Bishop's Palace estate, home to the Boleyn family, and later became the residence of the author Bulwer-Lytton, who wrote *The Last Days of Pompeii* there. It also briefly housed the exiled French Emperor, Napoleon III. [45]

Apart from the short-lived Glasgow United YMCA football team in the mid-1880s, there were very few Scottish football clubs with explicitly Protestant religious origins. One contributing factor was the ongoing opposition within certain factions of Scottish Presbyterianism to organised sport. Although Glasgow YMCA played a match against Queen's Park, Scotland's oldest club—founded by privately educated young professionals—its brief existence may have been curtailed by resistance from the Scottish Presbyterian Church. Such hostility had precedents. For instance, in 1853 the Stirling-based evangelist Peter Drummond published a tract entitled *Race, Games and Balls*, which denounced local sports as distractions from religious life. As football developed, concerns about professionalism and gambling persisted. It was not until 1908 that Protestant churches in Glasgow established the Glasgow and District Church League.[46]

In contrast, the Catholic Church in Scotland actively supported at least three clubs that later joined the Scottish League: Hibernian, Dundee United, and Glasgow Celtic. In my previous book, *Everton: The Fans*, I explained why, unlike in Glasgow, the Catholic Church played no role in the formation of Everton or Liverpool.[47] Secularisation in Liverpool was so profound that even the original *Liverpool Catholic Boys* team has been renamed *Merseyside Boys*.[48]

In Scotland, the success of Catholic clubs in Edinburgh and Dundee inspired two Catholic priests living in the East End of Glasgow to establish a football club. Unlike the Protestant church-affiliated clubs in England, the Scottish Catholic clubs were explicitly sectarian in nature. In 1875, Canon Edward Hannon, founder of Hibernian FC, included a clause in the club's constitution stating that all players must be practising Catholics. This clause was dropped in 1883. In Glasgow, in 1887, Brother Walfrid and local builder John Glass formed the *Glasgow Celtic Football and Athletic Club*. Walfrid, a member of the Marist Order, was involved in providing free school meals for Irish Catholic children in Glasgow's East End, partly to prevent them from seeking help from Protestant-run soup kitchens that might lead to conversion. Establishing football teams allowed the church to raise funds for these meal programmes through ticket sales.[49] The following year, Walfrid, Glass, and several volunteers built a stadium for the new club.[50] The increased revenue enabled the club to hire professional players, arguably diluting its original charitable ethos. In its first published balance sheet in 1889, 11 per cent of revenue was allocated to charitable donations—

many non-denominational—the highest proportion of any club in the UK at the time. By 1893, however, this figure had fallen below 1 per cent, and none was directed to Brother Walfrid's feeding schemes.[51] The extent to which professionalism weakened the link between religion and football will be explored further in Chapter 4.

Hibernian FC, founded in 1875 in Edinburgh by Canon Edward Hannon, was originally named after the Roman term for Ireland. It was established as an Irish Catholic club by famine survivors and formed as an offshoot of the Catholic Young Men's Society. Initially excluded from local and national leagues due to a ban on Irish teams, Hibernian relied on invitational matches, with proceeds reinvested in community projects through the church. Over time, they welcomed players of all faiths and were eventually admitted to the major Scottish leagues.[52]

The origins of Dundee United trace back to the short-lived club Dundee Harp, formed in 1879 to represent the city's Irish Roman Catholic population. It drew players from the Catholic parishes of St Andrew's and St Joseph's. Despite defeating Aberdeen Rovers 35–0 in 1885, Dundee Harp were denied the world scoring record because Arbroath beat Bon Accord 36–0 on the same day. Although the referee originally believed Harp had scored 37, he was corrected by one of the club's own officials. Harp's financial struggles led to suspension by the Scottish Football Association in the 1890s. A new club, *Dundee Hibernian*, emerged in 1909, playing at Tannadice Park and composed largely of former Harp players. This club eventually became *Dundee United* in 1923.[53]

Unlike in England, non-Catholic clubs in Scotland were seldom founded by local churches. Glasgow Rangers was formed by four teenage boys who conceived the idea while walking through West End Park (now Kelvingrove Park).[54] However, over time, the club became closely associated with Scottish Protestantism, particularly during the chairmanship of John Ure Primrose between 1912 and 1923. Bill Murray attributes the origins of Rangers' anti-Catholic signing policy to manager Bill Struth from 1920. Both Struth and Ure Primrose recognised the financial advantages of appealing to a Protestant fan base in their rivalry with Celtic. The policy may have also been influenced by the migration of Northern Irish Protestants to work in the Govan shipyards. Murray argues that Rangers adopted the hiring practices of Protestant-owned businesses in the area, which prioritised co-religionists. While there was some initial ambiguity—Struth is believed to have wanted to sign a Catholic player, but faced opposition from within the squad—by the 1940s, the policy was firmly established and unchallenged by either the press or the Scottish football authorities.[55]

This discriminatory policy lasted until 1989, when the club signed Mo Johnston, a Catholic and former Celtic player who had been expected to re-sign for Celtic but was offered better terms by Rangers.[56] Since then, Rangers have signed numerous Catholic players and even employed Catholic managers. By the early 2000s, Rangers occasionally had more Catholics in the squad than Celtic, including both the manager and captain.[57]

However, sectarian chanting remains an issue at both Rangers and Celtic. Sectarian attacks continue to occur in the city and tend to increase before or after Old Firm matches. A 2006 audit by the Crown Office found that 33 per cent of all religiously aggravated crimes in Scotland could be linked to football.[58] Professor David Morrow, who chaired an independent advisory group on tackling sectarianism in Scotland, summarised the changing relationship between religion and sport:

In a time when religion is less important in society, it is almost as if it has become part of the identity of football in Scotland. In a sense, sectarianism now is a way of behaving rather than a way of believing.[59]

It is important to note that religious sectarianism and football are not confined to Scotland. In 1949, the best-supported Catholic team in Northern Ireland, Belfast Celtic, withdrew from the Irish League due to violence against their players following their annual Boxing Day match against staunchly Protestant Linfield.[60] Since the 1985–86 season, another major Catholic nationalist club in Northern Ireland, Derry City, has played in the Republic's League of Ireland. The Northern Ireland national team has traditionally drawn support from the Protestant and Unionist community, while many Catholics and Nationalists have supported the Republic of Ireland team. However, following the 1998 Good Friday Agreement, the Irish Football Association launched the *Football for All* campaign to help eliminate sectarianism from the game. In 2006, the success of this campaign appeared to be recognised when Northern Irish fans were awarded the prestigious European Football Supporters Award for promoting a friendly atmosphere at matches. In 2016, both Northern Ireland and Republic of Ireland fans received the Grand Vermeil medal of Paris for exemplary sportsmanship during Euro 2016.[61]

In the 1920s, some Glasgow Rangers players explicitly identified with muscular Christian values. For instance, Alan Morton, who played for both Rangers and Scotland, became the Glaswegian equivalent of Scottish evangelical Olympic athlete Eric Liddell. Like Liddell, Morton supported D. P. Thomson's Glasgow Students Evangelistic Union. In 1926, during one of their meetings, a letter from Morton was read aloud that expressed clear muscular Christian ideals:

We are all playing a game – the game of life. How are we playing? Do we play the game like the sons of a King? If not, we should be, as all are sons of the King of Kings. A better captain than Jesus we cannot possibly get. It is therefore up to every sportsman to follow the captain's lead, so that in our everyday life our actions will show whose we are and whom we serve.[62]

The closest other Scottish clubs have come to religious origins is in their names: St Johnstone and St Mirren are named after Saint John the Baptist and Saint Mirin respectively.[63] [64]

A classic example of an English church-based club is Queens Park Rangers. The club originated from a Boys' Brigade unit set up by St Jude's Church on Lancefield Street, on the fringes of the Shaftesbury Park Estate – a community built on the same temperance principles as Bournville in Birmingham and Port Sunlight on the Wirral. The Boys' Brigade was founded in Glasgow in 1883 by Sir William Alexander Smith and was deeply rooted in the principles of muscular Christianity. Its aim was to develop Christian manliness through semi-military discipline, religious teaching, gymnastics and summer camps.[65] In 1888, Smith argued that the Brigade could dispel the widespread belief that religion was weak and feminine by appealing to a boy's imagination and instilling in him the *esprit de corps* of a soldier.[66] Founding football clubs was a natural progression from these ideals, though opposition from Protestant churches in Scotland meant that the first Glasgow Boys' Brigade football knock-out tournament was not organised until 1890.[67]

In West London, these values were put into practice by John Macdonald, the son of a Scottish emigrant. Raised on the Queens Park Estate, he attended the local board school where he developed a passion for football. As a teenager, Macdonald joined the St Jude's Boys' Brigade, which eventually formed a football team. With the vicar's permission, the club was founded and played its first match in 1886. Within a few months, it merged with Christ Church Rovers, another church-based team. To create a sense of unity, the club was renamed Queens Park Rangers, as most players lived on the Queens Park Estate.[68]

Appropriately for a church-founded team, Southampton are nicknamed *The Saints*. They were originally known as Southampton St Mary's, after the church that formed the club. When the team moved to the St Mary's Stadium in 2001, it was fitting, as it stood close to the original St Mary's Church which founded the club in 1885.

The club's formation was driven by the curate of St Mary's and leader of the Young Men's Association, Arthur Sole, and the rector of St Mary's, Canon Basil Wilberforce, the grandson of abolitionist William Wilberforce. Despite his privileged background, Wilberforce was a strong advocate of muscular Christianity. Educated at Eton and Exeter College, Oxford, he chose to work in a deprived inner-city parish, championing abstentionism and supporting schemes to discourage young men from turning to alcohol. In 1885, Sole and Wilberforce met with members of the St Mary's YMA cricket team to form the St Mary's Young Men's Association Football Club, which became Southampton FC in 1897.[69]

On an August evening in 1882, a group of teenage boys from the Hotspur Cricket Club met under a lamp post near the junction of Tottenham High Road and Park Lane to discuss forming a football club. The club's name honoured Sir Henry Percy (Harry Hotspur), whom some had learned about in history classes. Founding members Robert Buckle, Sam Casey, and John Anderson wanted to continue playing sport during the winter.[70] The church connection was established the following year when, after facing bullying on their pitch on Tottenham Marshes, some of the boys approached their Bible class teacher, John Ripsher, of All Hallows Church.[71] Ripsher became the club's first president and treasurer and helped secure a series of headquarters following multiple evictions. His dedication ensured the club's survival, and in 2007, Tottenham officials honoured him with a headstone on his previously unmarked grave in Dover, where he had died in a workhouse.[72]

In the 1884–85 season, the club changed its name to Tottenham Hotspur, having frequently been confused with another club, London Hotspur. That same season, they were again evicted from their YMCA headquarters when a council member was accidentally struck by a soot-covered football. Ripsher appealed to his vicar, the Reverend Alexander Wilson, who agreed to host the club at the Young Men's Church of England Society in Tottenham, on the condition that the boys attended All Hallows Church services every Wednesday evening. Wilson, a committed muscular Christian, had served as secretary of the Church of England National Society for Promoting the Education of the Poor and had established many schools in deprived areas. The arrangement lasted for two years until the boys began prioritising card games over church attendance, resulting in another eviction. Ripsher once again came to the rescue, securing premises at the Red House Coffee Palace, next to the site where White Hart Lane would later be built.[73]

Another English club with ecclesiastical roots is Swindon Town. The club's formation was led by the curate of Christ Church, Swindon, William Baker Pitt, an active member of the local YMCA. He sought to expand its influence by creating a football club. At the time, Swindon was socially divided between the old town, where Christ Church was located, and the new town, largely populated by Great Western Railway workers. In 1879, Pitt met with young railway workers and founded Swindon Town Football Club. The club's most famous early player, Harold Fleming, was deeply religious and refused to play on Good Friday or Christmas Day. His exemplary sportsmanship was shaped by his Christian faith.[74]

The Welsh club The New Saints was renamed in 2006 after Saint Oswald, who has a strong historical connection to the English town of Oswestry, where the club is based.[75]

Christianity continues to influence modern football clubs. Since the mid-twentieth century, club chaplains have been appointed. Currently, eleven Premier League clubs and fifty-five Football League clubs have chaplains.[76] According to Sports Chaplaincy UK, a sports chaplain provides personal support to those in the profession, many of whom come from abroad, and addresses both the mental and physical toll of elite sport.[77]

Football chaplains can also provide spiritual support for fans. At Charlton Athletic, chaplain Matt Baker oversees a memorial garden with views of the pitch and conducts 10–15 services a year for the scattering of ashes.[78]

Everton FC was unique in the Premier League in having St Luke's Anglican Church located in one corner of its Goodison Road stadium. Although the church did not found the club, which was established by St Domingo Methodist New Connexion Methodist Church, it pre-dates Goodison Park by nine years. Over time, St Luke's has formed close ties with the club. In 1994, parish vicar Harry Ross was appointed club chaplain. He became a leading figure in the Everton Former Players' Foundation, looking after former players in need and conducting funeral services for figures such as Harry Catterick and Andy King.[79] In 2024, following Ross's death in 2019, the Reverend Lyn Davidson, Priest-in-Charge of St Luke's, was appointed as the new chaplain. Earlier that year, she led the memorial service for former striker Kevin Campbell. Davidson was expected to play a significant role in overseeing Everton's transition from the old Goodison Park, helping to maintain a sense of continuity with the club's historic home.[80]

Some Northern Irish clubs have also, relatively recently, displayed openly religious messages at their grounds. Between 1995 and 2010, Glentoran had a sign with *Jesus* on it, before it was removed to make space for advertising.[81] Portadown also had a sign reading *Life without Jesus makes no sense* along the side of their ground.[82]

The occasional owners of football clubs today also appear to be motivated by religion. American Mormon Alan Pace became chairman of Burnley in 2020. His company, ALK Capital, has an all-Mormon board. Pace's father was a Mormon missionary who came to the north-west of England aged 19 and later urged his son to follow suit. This made a strong impression on Pace and appears to be one of the reasons he encouraged the company to take over Burnley.[83]

Some chairmen hold strong religious principles that affect how they fulfil their roles. Ross County chairman Roy MacGregor, when he first took over the club, refused to watch games played on Sundays. He is a member of the Free Church of Scotland, which traditionally maintains a strict interpretation of keeping the Sabbath as a holy day. However, although he remains opposed to Sunday football, he had a change of heart and, in March 2016, attended the Scottish League Cup Final against Hibernian. He stressed that he lived his religion seven days a week, not just on Sundays.[84]

There are still some teams founded by churches today. In 2020, the Reverend Pouya Heidari, a former professional player from Iran, formed the first Church of England team in modern times. It is composed of 18 vicars from across the country. The team coach is former Sunderland player Maurice Hepworth, a member of the Christian charity *Faith in Football*.[85]

Currently, there are 24 nationwide contemporary Christian leagues in the UK, including one in Norfolk. Formed in 1978, it had 58 teams participating by 2011. The league also includes youth teams. [86] Another example is the South Manchester and Cheshire Christian League, founded in 1999. Initially planned as a six-team league, it has since expanded significantly. Religious practices include both teams standing in the centre circle while someone from the home side leads a short prayer. It now has 28 teams competing in three leagues.[87]

Since 1959, Southend-on-Sea has had its own Catholic team, Catholic United FC. It was set up to represent the town's

Catholic population. In 1968, the club adopted green and white hoops after receiving a set of kits from Glasgow Celtic. [88]

In 2002, former professional footballer Linvoy Primus and others established the organisation *Faith + Football* in Portsmouth. As Christians, they aimed to serve their local communities by using football to support young people and families. It offers a range of community, educational and overseas programmes. The organisation has since expanded to Plymouth and Cambridge, where they have also created children's football leagues.[89]

However, not all Christian league teams consistently demonstrate Christian attitudes. In 2015, Pye Green Towers FC were disbanded after a match in the West Midlands Christian League against Selly Oak Methodists. This followed accusations that players had chanted *we're racist and that's the way we like it*, apparently mimicking racist chants made by Chelsea fans in Paris, within earshot of the black referee. The team's captain reportedly apologised profusely to the referee before kick-off.[90]

Other faiths in the UK have also founded lesser-known football clubs. In 1919, the St George's Settlement Synagogue in the East End of London established several football teams. In 1937, Maccabi GB was founded as a Jewish charity in response to Jews being excluded from mainstream sport. In 1957, its team began competing in the Southern League. In 1985, Maccabi GB launched a Southern League for Jewish players in London and Essex. It has since grown steadily and now includes over 40 teams across three divisions.[91]

In Wolverhampton in 1966, Punjabi FC was established as the first Sikh-based football club in the country.[92] Also in Wolverhampton, Punjabi Wolves were founded in 1954. They are widely recognised as the largest organised group of ethnic football supporters in the world, with a membership exceeding 500.[93]

There have also been several Muslim football clubs established. AHF, a juniors club in Blackburn, is run by the Abu Hanifah Foundation, which emphasises a progressive interpretation of Islam. It aims to nurture well-rounded young people who will contribute positively to wider British society—an uncanny echo of earlier muscular Christianity. Although its teams are primarily Muslim, they are open to all faiths and include girls' teams.[94]

One Muslim girls' team in London is Sisterhood FC. It was set up to provide Muslim girls with a safe environment to play football. The club began when one of its founders recruited hijab-wearing girls at university to attend a training session. The team plays other London clubs and ensures respectful conduct, such as always shaking hands with the opposition. The club is growing and aims to inspire young girls growing up in the Muslim faith.[95]

A campaign led by Muslim girl Asmahan Mansour, who had been banned from playing a football match in Canada, contributed to FIFA's 2014 decision to lift its ban on Muslim women wearing head coverings, following a seven-year campaign.[96] This development has complicated FIFA's enforcement of its ban on religious messages on player attire, which will be discussed in Chapter 4. However, a vote by the French Senate in February 2025 to ban all religious symbols, including the headscarf, from sports competitions shows that the issue remains unresolved.[97] That same month, news emerged from Bangladesh of Islamists forcing the cancellation of three women's football matches in the north of the country.[98]

In his research on young Muslim boys at an independent Islamic school in the Midlands, Samaya Farooq has identified a muscular Islamic set of beliefs surrounding the playing of football. Some of his interviews with the boys reveal religious ideals uncannily similar to those of nineteenth-century muscular Christianity:

The rules of sport are all about controlling yourself... controlling, disciplining your nafs (the psyche or negative urges) as opposed to letting it control you by getting angry and punching or kicking someone... this is important if we wanna become good Muslim men, 'cos Allah rewards discipline.[99]

The next chapter will examine how religion has inspired the growth of football in other countries.

CHAPTER 3

RELIGION AND FOOTBALL OUTSIDE THE UK

The spread of football from the UK in the late nineteenth and early twentieth centuries was largely fueled by trade, although religion also played a significant role. Paradoxically, in the white parts of the British Empire, other sports became gradually dominant, such as ice hockey in Canada, Rugby Union in South Africa and New Zealand, and Aussie Rules Football in Australia. Here, there is some evidence of the religious influence in their spread. Tony Collins has argued that the spread of Rugby to the empire was itself a product of muscular Christianity.

Thanks to the importance of muscular Christianity to the British Empire, rugby soon became the hegemonic code of football in the 'White Dominions' of the British Empire. Even the distinctive form of football played in the Australian colony of Victoria, which became known as Australian Rules football, was originally based on Rugby School's rules.[1]

Interestingly, some of the Australian rules football teams have also been influenced by religious divisions. S. Alomes has outlined the history of the Protestant Churches' league in the northern suburbs of Essendon in the 1950s and 60s. He also commented on the significant Jewish support for St. Kilda.[2]

Tony Collins has argued that a key factor in the spread of Rugby was that it was the sport practised in the book Tom Brown's Schooldays, which was so infused with the values of muscular Christianity.[3]

Football spread much more quickly in non-Empire countries in Europe and South America. This was initially through trade, for example, Lancashire textile workers first played football in 1866 in the Netherlands, whilst in Denmark, there were early reports of British sailors playing the game. In Spain, British workers for Rio Tinto influenced the creation of the country's first club, Recreativo de Huelva. Later, miners from Sunderland and sailors from Southampton played a crucial role in the formation and colours of Athletic Bilbao. British sailors appear to have been a driving force of the game in Latin America. One possible religiously inspired figure to set up a Spanish football club was the Swiss evangelical Protestant and Accountant, Hans Gamper. In 1889, he founded FC Barcelona and helped football become a central part of the new culture of the rising Catalan middle class.[4]

There was also a possible influence of the English private school system, as it is believed that FC Barcelona's club colours were taken from the rugby team of Merchant Taylors' school in Crosby, Merseyside. The school regarded sport as a major part of a young man's development in the spirit of muscular Christianity. Two brothers who had attended the school, Arthur and Ernest Witty, were heavily involved in the formation of the club. [5]

In many countries in Latin America, the British set up schools where football was practised. At these schools, football was often developed by 'football evangelists' such as Charles Miller in São Paulo, Leslie Poole in Montevideo and Alexander Watson Hutton in Buenos Aires. They were all inspired by the values of muscular Christianity.[6]

In Argentina, trading links had led to the setting up of British schools. Alexander Watson Hutton set up the crucial one in Buenos Aires. He was initially employed at St. Andrew's School, the oldest English school in the country. He was from Glasgow and had been educated at Edinburgh University when the Edinburgh University Association Football Club was set up in 1878.[7] He fell out with St. Andrew's School over its lack of playing fields and gymnasiums. Watson subsequently founded his own school, the English High School. At the new school, football would be central to the curriculum, and this would set the tone for elite schools across the city. He organised the first mini leagues in Buenos Aires in 1891 and two years later, the Argentine Association Football League was formed, which has lasted to this day. This was the first competitive football league to be contested outside of Britain. Watson would be known as the 'father of Argentinian football'.[8]

In Brazil, Charles Miller founded the São Paulo Athletic Club in 1895 and the regional league, the Campeonato Paulista, which is still contested by São Paulo's top teams. He is regarded as the 'father of football' in Brazil. He learned to play football in a public school in Southampton run by the Reverend George Ellaby, called Banister's Court. In a corner of the estate was a picturesque corner known as the Dell, later to become the ground of Southampton Football Club.[9] He played football for his school, his county and even a few games for Southampton.

In 1894, he went back to São Paulo; his mother was Brazilian. He took with him two leather footballs, some kit and a copy of the Hampshire FA rules in his suitcase. It was while playing cricket at the São Paulo Athletic Club that he suggested to a few others that they should try football; thus, the football club was formed.

By 1902, following the arrival of German immigrants and with the assistance of American students, Miller established the Campeonato Paulista. He also proposed the name 'Corinthians' to the first president of Sport Club Corinthians Paulista, now one of the country's major teams, taking inspiration from an English side Corinthians, renowned for playing the game in the spirit of muscular Christianity, with its emphasis on sportsmanship and fair play.[10]

Miller himself commented in 1904, after refereeing a 20-a-side match of small boys, on how the game was spreading to the lower classes. This was later enhanced by the rise of factory teams.[11]

In Uruguay, the British School was opened in 1885 by Thomas Ashe and was directly modelled on the ideas of Alexander Watson Hutton. Employed at the school from its inception was its Cambridge-educated master of English, William Leslie Poole. The values of muscular Christianity were evident in the ethos of the school outlined in an interview with Hutton in 1899 – ... *they are not wise men, but capable men, with precise notions of chivalry and the word.* [12]

An alumnus from the school, Henry Candid Lichtenburger, founded the first football club in Uruguay, the Club Albion. This was strictly for Uruguayans. However, it was Poole who organised and professionalised sport in the country. He allowed access to foreigners and people from all backgrounds. He also became president of the Uruguayan Football Association after serving as both a player and a referee. Albion went on to win the Uruguayan league in its first season of 1900 but was superseded by Wanderers.[13] They also became the first Uruguayan team to tour Argentina in 1896 and, in 1899, built the first Uruguayan stadium to be used solely for football. It had a capacity of 1,000. Initially, they were the driving force of Uruguayan football, winning eighteen of nineteen fixtures in 1896, but by 1908, it faded, and the club was relegated to Division 2.[14]

British schools also played a key role in developing the sport in Chile. It was first played at the Mackay and Sutherland school in Valparaiso. It was run by two Scots, Peter Mackay and George Sutherland. The first Chilean football club was set up at the school in 1882, and a decade later, the first major Chilean club was formed in Valparaíso by David Scott.

Initially, it was totally British, with a significant Scottish component. In 1895, Scott formed the Football Association of Chile, and football spread to the capital, Santiago. The early rivalries were between the mainly foreign-based clubs from Valparaiso and the Chilean-based clubs in Santiago.[15]

In some parts of Latin America, the Catholic church was instrumental in the development of football. For example, in Costa Rica, after the Catholic church lost power in the late nineteenth century and its political party was suppressed, some priests were able to reassert their power by organising football associations in numerous towns. One of the first was set up by Father Porras in San Pedro de Poas.[16]

Ireland presented a unique example of Catholic muscular Christianity opposing the spread of the British version of football and, instead, supporting locally developed variants such as Gaelic football. David Goldblatt sees the Irish Catholic church, exemplified by Archbishop Croke in the late nineteenth century, as being sympathetic to the development of Gaelic football, founded in 1844, as a nationalist alternative to Association football. The close links with Irish Catholicism were sealed by the naming of Ireland's main GAA stadium after the archbishop. Goldblatt also emphasises that the Gaelic Athletic Association shared many similar values with British Public Schools, which were the major vehicle in promoting association football:

The GAA's equation of national self-consciousness and national well-being displayed the same belief in the connections between ethnicity, race athleticism and the body that underwrote the games ethic in that most British of institutions – the public school.[17]

Arthur Griffith's Sinn Féin movement saw Gaelic sports as the ideal vehicle for mobilising young men to the republican cause:

The main duty of the GAA is the cultivation of the Irish physique generally through the national and natural medium of our games.[18]

In Italy, the Catholic church wasn't just opposed to football; as a result of a papal decree of 1868, it opposed its members from participating in political activity, which also included sports clubs. As a result, Italian football clubs were formed through businessmen in the northern cities with strong British links. A good example in Turin was Eduardo de Bosio, who traded with Britain and brought back a football in 1887 when the first game was played. From his circle, FC Torino was formed.

Gradually, the Catholic church in Italy started to embrace the game through fears that modern sports were born in Victorian England, and young people would be affected by 'Protestant' values if the Catholic church wasn't involved. This culminated in 1891 with Pope Leo XIII passing the *Rerum Novarum*, which was designed to create a Catholic space which would have the support of the masses. This open letter to all Italian clerics changed the church's attitude to sport and strengthened pre-existing Catholic sporting organisations like the Salesians, who had set up sporting structures under Don Giovanni Bosco since the 1840s. It also eventually led to the setting up of the Catholic Sports Associations in 1906, which helped foster the growth of football.[19]

In Germany, the Catholic and Protestant churches were initially opposed to games of any sort. The German game initially started in Braunschweig when two teachers ordered a ball from England. It later spread via trade to cities like Bremen and Hanover.[20] One of the teachers in Braunschweig was certainly imbued with the spirit of muscular Christianity, Dr. Conrad Koch. He had studied Theology and Philology, and through his travels in England, he became a follower of Thomas Arnold at Rugby School and wanted to turn sporting and team-building exercises in the right direction.

He was especially impressed with Arnold's system of self-government, where older pupils are given the responsibility of acting as leaders to the younger ones. He and a fellow teacher started the first game in Germany when they threw the newly purchased ball to a group of students at the Martino Katharineum High School in Braunschweig in the autumn of 1874. The following year, Koch published his *FuBlummelei,* which provided guidelines and regulations for the new game. [21]

There is also some evidence that football started in the same year in Dresden by the English Reverend Bowden. This influenced a tour with students at Oxford University the following year.[22]

Another teacher who founded a German club was Walter Bensemann. The club that would eventually become FV Karlsruhe was created in 1888. Bensemann was also influenced by the values of British schools, as he had taught languages at English private schools.[23] Although the game wasn't founded by the church in Germany, at least one club does have an indirect church influence in its foundation.

Borussia Dortmund was founded by young men unhappy with the Catholic church-sponsored Trinity Youth club under the stern and unsympathetic eye of Father Dewald, the local parish priest. The young men met in a room of a local pub, where they blocked the door when Father Dewald attempted to enter. They called their club Borussia after a beer brewed in a local brewery.[24]

As in Germany, English schools had a significant influence on the development of the game in Denmark. Many wealthy Danes sent their sons to top English schools in the nineteenth century. This meant that football appeared in Danish schools as early as 1877. In the previous year, four men founded KB Copenhagen as a multi-sports society, which adopted Association rules football in 1879. In 1889, the Danish Ballgame Union was formed, which is the world's oldest national football association outside of Britain.[25]

However, in Portugal, like in Italy, the Catholic church was worried that Protestant dominated organisations like the YMCA would have a monopoly on sports education. The YMCA was at the peak of its power in the years following the Great War when it organised the Inter-Allies games in Joinville, France, which attracted 1415 athletes from the Allied powers, including Catholic Italy and Portugal. This caused particular concern in Portugal because, unlike in Italy, there were no Catholic sporting organisations.

Consequently, in May 1922, the Sixth Congress of Portuguese Catholic youth voted to use sport to strengthen the

Catholic presence in the country. The values of muscular Christianity were very clearly underpinning this move, as an extract from a Catholic journal suggests, when addressing the goals of physical education, which were – *modelling the morale and the bodies of the new generations to reinforce the Portugal of tomorrow.* But it wasn't until 1938-39 that a Portuguese championship was set up. But it was under the rule of Marcelo Caetano from 1941 that football really spread.[26]

As in Portugal, the Catholic church played a significant role in the development of football in Belgium. A young Irishman, Cyril Bernard Morrogh, is said to have bought a ball in 1863 and played with his friends at the Josephite College of Melle, just outside of Ghent. The Josephites were seen at the time as a progressive group within the Catholic church which were supportive of the ideals of physical health. The game became popular in schools, and there is some evidence that it was encouraged by the Catholic church as a way of combining healthy minds and healthy bodies. This is another example of how muscular Catholicism fostered football.[27]

In France, football appears to have been brought by an English vicar, the interestingly named Reverend George Washington. In 1872, he and a group of Oxbridge-educated ex-pats set up Havre FC in the Normandy port of Le Havre. From here, the Brits exported the game to Paris, where they set up several sporting clubs which played football.[28]

The first football club to be founded in continental Europe was the Lausanne Football and Cricket Club in Switzerland, founded in 1860 by English students studying at private schools in the area.[29] Muscular Christian values were instrumental to the spread of football in Switzerland when it became established at schools in the 1880s. Its values

46

emphasised adherence to the rules, teamwork and the shaping of boys into disciplined and healthy men. This code was directly adopted from the British public schools. In German-speaking countries, it had a specific name: *Körpererziehung*.[30]

One of the earliest football clubs in Austria was the Jewish team Hakoah Vienna. The writer on Argentinian football, Jonathan Wilson, has even used the phrase muscular Judaism to describe their philosophy when referring to their South American tour in 1930.[31]

Hakoah was established in 1909, influenced by the Jewish philosopher Max Nordau's philosophy of muscular Judaism, which emphasised that a new Jewish character had to be forged based on mental and physical strength to achieve the goals of Zionism. Hakoah, whose name means strength in Hebrew, were renowned for its players decorating their uniforms with Jewish symbols such as the Star of David and adopting nicknames of Jewish military leaders like Bar Kochba.[32]

Football arrived in the Albanian city of Shkoder in the early twentieth century. Reputedly, in 1908, an Anglo-Maltese monk brought the game from Malta, where it had been firmly established by British sailors. It was played at the Catholic Xaverian School, where locals took an interest and spread the game to the rest of the country.[33]

The British Empire played a significant role in exporting football to the colonies. According to Richard Holt, the Sudan Political Service recruited entrants from 1899 primarily based on recommendations from Oxbridge dons. Of the 393 entrants to the administrative grade, seventy-one had fully representative sporting honours from Oxford or Cambridge, and many more had prominent sporting roles at the leading public schools.[34] So the values of muscular Christianity were firmly held by the administrators. These were aspects of what Brian Stoddart called *cultural power,* the set of ideas, beliefs, rules and conventions concerning social behaviour that were carried out throughout the empire.[35] Sport played a key role in the transmission of these values and in the development of social cohesion between the colonists and the native populations.[36] But missionary schools became the primary direct vehicle of exporting the sport.

For a variety of reasons previously discussed, football didn't gain a foothold among the white dominions. However, it was really in Black Africa that football was more successfully exported by the British through religion. A major vehicle for this was the missionary school. The colonial educationalist AG Fraser brought football to his school in Kampala, Uganda, in 1900 and then to the Gold Coast in 1903.

In Ghana, football was established in 1921 when two clubs came into existence. One was called Everton FC, a recreational club for the Kumasi Roman Catholic Mission school. The second club, Royals FC, was sponsored by the Wesleyan Mission School. The patronage of both clubs was strictly based on religion. Teichman Holy Stars, who still play in the Ghana league, belonged originally to the Teichman Roman Catholic church.[37] There is some evidence today that the Ghanaian church is still involved in promoting the game and creating gender inequalities within it.[38]

Football was introduced to Nigeria by a group of Jamaican Presbyterians who founded the Hope Waddell Training Institute. In 1902, the Reverend James Luke arrived as headmaster and brought a football with him. The first recorded game played by the pupils and teachers occurred on

June 15th, 1904, when the barefoot Nigerians beat a team from HMS Thistle 3-2.[39]

More recently, in 2007, the Pentecostal church has been instrumental in setting up the Lagos Mountain of Fire club, which now plays in the country's Premier League.[40] Football was crucially spread in Kenya by Scottish missionary Marion Stevenson. She regarded it as a morally improving sport, and in 1909, she played a part in arranging the first inter-school cup competition when a team from the Church Missionary Society in Kabete took on a team from the Church of Scotland mission in Thogoto. Later, the locals made the game their own.[41]

Malawi was another British African colony where missionaries played an important role in developing the game. As early as 1880, there is some evidence of football being played at the Blantyre Mission, founded by the Church of Scotland and named after David Livingstone's birthplace. However, the game took off at the Likoma Mission. In 1910, the Anglican missionaries there introduced a proper set of rules, which helped the game spread to the rest of the country. In 1938, James Frederick Sangala, who had been educated at the Blantyre Mission, helped set up the Shire Highlands African League.[42]

Football in Uganda was originally introduced by the missionaries George Lawrence Pilkington at the Mengo school in Kampala and Alexander Gordon Fraser at King's School in Budo. In 1909, Budo Old Boys became the first established club in the country. In 1922, Archdeacon Robert Walker established the African and Arab Football Association in Kampala.[43]

In French West Africa, football was rarely practised due to the greater separation between the colonial authorities and the Africans. However, in Brazzaville, Africans did play the game as it had been introduced by monks from the local Catholic mission who saw it as a positive counter to the negative effects of urban life on the local population.[44] The game was introduced following Mass on Sunday, after school or during holidays.[45]

In South Africa, one of the main reasons why football became the main sport of the indigenous black population was the role of mission schools and churches in converting the local population and encouraging it to play the game.[46] Mission schools, such as Lovedale, Healdtown and Zonnebloem, introduced sport to African students in the late nineteenth century.[47]

In India, the army was a vehicle for transmitting football to native Indians. In the late nineteenth century, it consisted of 65,000 British soldiers and 120,000 Indian sepoys. Through football, both could mix. For example, the winning team of the Fifty-Second Sikhs consisted of seven British and four Indian sepoys.[48] The main impetus for the founding of football clubs, however, came from the missionary schools. J.A. Mangan has shown how they encouraged the game in the late nineteenth century.

In 1891, an English missionary called Cecil Earle Tyndale-Biscoe took a football and his wife to the Church Missionary Society School in Srinagar, Kashmir. He saw sport as a means of tackling the social stigmas of the caste system and increasing the physical fitness of children who otherwise wouldn't be encouraged to gain physical strength.[49] After difficult beginnings, the sport prospered so much that by 1922, he was to witness an inter-class match refereed by a pupil. The players perfectly abided by the rules. Football is still popular in

Kashmir, and pupils at Tyndale-Biscoe School won an All-India tournament in Delhi in 2018. It's a fitting tribute to Tyndale-Biscoe's interpretation of muscular Christianity:

Bundles must be turned into boys by athletic exercises and athletic boys turned into manly citizens by continued acts of kindness.[50]

The main city under British influence to have founded football clubs was Calcutta. It remains the centre of Indian football to this day. In the late nineteenth century, Tony Mason has shown how, in Calcutta, the British schools taught football as a means of promoting a common cultural ground among disparate groups.[51] At the turn of the twentieth century, local football clubs were formed as a symbol of protest against British rule. This took on a particular role when they played British teams. The teams, to this day, continue to be segregated on religious grounds, with two Hindu teams, East Bengal and Mohun Bagan and one Muslim, Mohammedan Sporting Club.[52]

The first significant club to develop was Mohun Bagan, formed in 1889. It won its first title in 1904, and in 1909, it first played a British team. This was the 1st Middlesex Regiment, in a tournament previously closed to them, the IFA Shield. The British team won out on this occasion, but they came back two years later to beat the same team over two legs in the Semi-Final. They then won the trophy after defeating the East Yorkshire regiment 2-1 in the final. The match gained significant symbolic importance to the local Bengali population as this extract from a local newspaper indicates:

It fills every Indian with pride and joy to know that rice-eating, malaria-ridden, bare-footed Bengalis have got the better of beef-eating, Herculean, booted John Bull in that peculiarly English sport.[53]

The victory was sometimes referred to as *The Revenge of Plassey*, after the 1757 battle that established the East India Company's control over Bengal.[54]

When Mohammedan Sporting was formed a few years later, they brought a new level of professionalism to the game and repeatedly won the Calcutta league in the 1930s before becoming the first Indian team to win the prestigious Durand Cup in 1940.[55] East Bengal FC was formed later in 1920 after an immigrant from East Bengal was so incensed by discrimination against his fellow East Bengalis at his club Jorabagan that he formed a separate club. After the partition in 1947, many Hindu refugees came to the city from East Bengal, which later became Bangladesh. The club received an enormous boost in support from them and started to challenge Mohun Bagan for dominance. They are now the two best-supported teams in the city.[56]

The British Evangelist Theodore Leighton Pennell originally introduced football in Pakistan in the 1890s. It was in the missionary school of Bannu in the Northwest Frontier, a few miles to the south of Afghanistan, that the game was set up.[57] In the Pakistani Premier League, there is even a team called Muslim FC based in Chaman. They were formed in 2010 in Balochistan, the most football-supporting region of the country. Their rivalry with the local team, Afghan Chaman, regularly attracts the biggest national crowds in the country for a football match.[58]

Another Scottish pioneer of international football was James George Scott. Whilst teaching at the Missionary School of St John's College in Rangoon, he introduced the sport to Myanmar. He assembled a team from his college and another one from the port of Moulmein.[59]

There is evidence in the then Portuguese colony of Goa that football was brought through the Catholic church. This was initially in the form of a British priest, Father William Robert Lyons. He founded St. Joseph's school at Siolim in 1883. Soon, other headmasters in the town became convinced of the value of playing football. In 1893, the private English school in Assolna started playing the game under the leadership of its Senior master, Antonio Francisco de Souza. The Rachel seminary, which was the primary training centre for priests, also started playing the game, although they were later banned from playing by the Bishop of the East Indies.[60]

However, the game was maintained by the pre-existing village organisations, which were closely allied with local priests. The game thrived into the twentieth century with Goan-wide tournaments being set up. The first one in 1925 was in front of a crowd of 4,000. For Scottish historian James Mills, the way that local priests adopted the game at this time was similar to how Scottish Catholic priests had helped form the Catholic clubs in Scotland. He believes that the way in which the Goan Catholic church had become indigenised was crucial in the spread of football by appearing to be distinct from the Portuguese colonial authorities. When the Goan economy stagnated in the early twentieth century, many Goans moved to nearby Bombay, where they formed Goan football clubs.[61]

Within Europe, part of the colonial empire was the island of Cyprus. Football was introduced there by an Anglican priest, Frank Darvall Newham. In 1900, he became Director of Education for the island. In the same year, he founded the English School in Nicosia. The English curriculum included football, and the first games on the island took place in the school. By 1912, the then Canon Newham introduced Cyprus' first football cup competition.[62]

Outside of the colonial empires, missionary schools also introduced the game to Tibet. From 1869, the British government urged Moravian missionaries in western Tibet to set up schools, but the local population were fearful that the schools would be used for military recruitment, so the missionaries started to organise football matches to reassure locals and attract more students.[63]

In the Middle East, football was originally introduced to Palestine by missionary schools like St George's, which took up the game in 1908. Under the British mandate following World War I, the authorities wanted to open the game up to both Arabs and Jews, so clubs like Jerusalem Sports Club were set up in 1920, open to both. An Islamic Sports Club was set up in Jaffa, which played football in 1926, and an Orthodox Christian club open to Arabs was also set up there.[64]

Maccabi Tel Aviv was originally set up in 1906 in Jaffa. It became the first Jewish team to compete in the Palestinian leagues when it changed its name in 1922 with the creation of the new city of Tel Aviv. It took the Star of David as its emblem to represent the Jewish people. It went on, after the creation of the state of Israel in 1948, to become the most successful club in the country, having never been relegated from the Israeli Premier League and qualifying for the Champions' League group stages.

The name Maccabbi comes from a tribe of Jewish rebel warriors who took control over Judea in 167 BC.[65] Also in Israel, the club Beitar Jerusalem was founded by the Beitar Revisionist Zionist movement. It remains the only Israeli Premier League club never to have signed an Arab player, and its fans are renowned for their anti-Arab racism and religious bigotry.[66] When the club signed two Muslim players from Chechnya in 2013, arsonists torched the club's trophy room. Some of their fans were also arrested after singing racist chants against the players.[67]

More recently, in Italy, the Catholic church has long halted its opposition to football. In the Vatican City, the first club was formed by the staff at the Vatican Museums in the mid-1960s. The first Vatican league was formed in 1972, and in the same year, a Vatican City national team was also formed. In 2007, a mini World Cup was created, the Clericus Cup, from Rome's seminaries and ecclesiastical colleges. Recently, Popes have been notoriously enthusiastic about the game, starting with Pope John Paul II at the end of the 20th century and culminating with Pope Francis.[68]

Many football clubs in Catholic countries have chapels built in their stadia. One of the most famous is the one in FC Barcelona's Camp Nou stadium. It was built a few months after the inauguration of the stadium in 1957, when two of the men who carried the statue of the Virgin of Montserrat into the stadium for the inauguration ceremony were involved in a serious car accident. After their recovery, it was decided to build a chapel in the players' tunnel by way of a thanksgiving offering. Since then, inauguration masses are held with the entire team before the start of each season and in 1982, a club record attendance of 120,000 was set when Pope John Paul II held a solemn mass there. In 2025, it was announced that the newly redeveloped stadium will also incorporate a chapel in its old place.[69]

In Brazil, Vasco De Gama has a chapel the size of a church inside its stadium.[70]

There are still occasionally football clubs abroad founded by Christianity. In 1980, a Christian missionary team was formed in South Korea called Hallelujah FC. It was founded by Choi Soon-Young, a Korean businessman and President of the Korean Football Association. It consisted exclusively of Christian players and coaches. The team won the 1983 K League but went amateur in 1986 to focus on missionary work. It was disbanded in 1998 due to the Asian financial crisis.[71]

There are also some clubs owned by Christian groups. In 1996, Amazulu FC in Zimbabwe was set up by a group of Seventh-day Adventists. However, despite winning the country's premier Soccer league in 2003, they were thrown out of the league in 2005 for refusing to play a match on a Saturday as they recognise it as the sabbath and must therefore be kept special. Up till 2005, they had managed to come to arrangements with other clubs to reschedule Saturday fixtures. However, in 2005, Motor Action FC refused to do this and Amazulu were thrown out of the league and subsequently went out of existence.[72]

Islam has been involved with football clubs for the last sixty years. In 1964, Al Ahed was set up in the southern suburbs of Beirut. It is primarily supported by the Shia Muslim population and is affiliated with Hezbollah, the Shia political party and militant group. In 1970, it changed its name to the Al Huda Islamic Club, but renamed itself again in 1992 to Al Ahed (The Covenant) as its leaders wanted it to have a Quranic meaning.[73] Also, in Lebanon, there is a team linked to the Sunni Muslim population, Al Ansar, and a predominantly Orthodox Christian club, Racing Beirut. [74]

In 2011, the Guardian sports journalist Darry Glendenning reported that the Muslim Brotherhood in Egypt had set up a team of their own to compete in the Egyptian league.[75] The move seemed to be inspired by the success of militant fans of the top Egyptian clubs Al Ahly SC and Al Zamalek SC in organising protests against the police and supporters of former president Hosni Mubarak. It also marked a desire for the Brotherhood to distance themselves from traditional clerical hostility to the game.[76] However, the club didn't get off the ground, and it wouldn't have been allowed under the military coup of 2013. There is also some evidence in Egypt of footballing discrimination against the minority Coptic Christian community. A report in 2018 identified twenty-five cases of Coptic Christian players being marginalised or discriminated against. This may have led to only six members of the community, despite forming ten per cent of the population, to have joined top-flight Egyptian clubs. Despite this report being sent to FIFA, by 2018, it still hadn't taken any action.[77]

In northern Iraq, specifically Iraqi Kurdistan, there are both separate Muslim and Christian teams. In the cities of Erbil and Qaraqosh, there were fifty-five amateur football teams, mainly comprising displaced Christians.

In the period of 2017-18, researchers partnered with Nineveh Governorate Council and a Christian NGO and conducted an experiment involving fifty-one Christian teams. They were told to accept an additional three players, who may or may not have been Christian. They found that in the six months after the intervention, Christians with Muslim teammates were more tolerant of them and on broader social issues, but this didn't apply generally to Muslim strangers.[78]

In another Islamic country, Iran, football has had a chequered history since the Islamic revolution in 1979.

Initially, the game was banned. Eventually, an Iranian team was formed, but it had to train abroad during the Iran/Iraq war of the 1980s. It made its global breakthrough at the 1998 World Cup in France when they beat the archenemy the United States. The mass celebrations in Tehran forced the authorities to be more accommodating to football. However, there have been ongoing problems in allowing women to watch the male game. There may also be religious conflicts with the national team.

For example, in 2016, Iran was playing South Korea on the evening of the religious holiday of Ashura. Iran's Football Association wanted to postpone the match, but FIFA objected. As a result, Iranian clerics instructed fans to don black clothing and refrain from clapping.

During the match, placards were presented and slogans were chanted in honour of Ashura; as a result, the Iranian FA were fined $53,000 by FIFA.[79]

Clearly, Christian missionaries in the late nineteenth century and the early twentieth century played a crucial role in influencing the spread of football through the non-white British Empire. The missionaries shared muscular Christian values, which were also held by British school masters who helped spread the game in South America.

However, here and in Europe, the main vehicle for the spread of football was the growing trade links between industrial Britain and the rest of the world. More recently, Islam, after initially being opposed to the game, has assisted its growth.

The next chapter will look at how, from the late nineteenth century onwards, religion gradually played a lesser role in football.

CHAPTER 4

THE DECLINING INFLUENCE OF RELIGION ON FOOTBALL

Although many English football clubs were founded by churches, their influence over the clubs was destined to be short-lived. Some sections of the church were adamantly opposed to football as late as 1982, as the following quote by a minister at a service for football indicates:

Exercise thyself into godliness, for bodily exercise profiteth little.[1]

Historically, the most obvious distancing of football from religion was in the way early English clubs gradually developed names to reflect their community rather than the churches which created them. St Domingo's, which was founded by Everton, lost its name within a year after becoming the best team in the area and recruiting from other church teams such as St. Peter's, St. Benedict's and the United Church team. Consequently, at a meeting in the Queens Hotel in December 1879, it was decided to rename the club Everton in recognition of the players from the wider community. [2]

Although Aston Villa was originally formed as Aston Villa Wesleyan Chapel in 1874, it's unclear when the term Wesleyan was dropped. However, by the 1880s, the term had been dropped. Aston was a recognisable district, and the club may have wanted to broaden its support. This was the pattern replicated at all the clubs founded by churches, so that within twenty years, usually less, none of these clubs retained their original church names.[3] The sociologist Jeffrey Cox saw church involvement with things like football as part of its moral influence on non-churchgoers. He sees this as a success of the late Victorian church, which only started to break down in the early twentieth century when the church reverted to concentrating on spiritual welfare and became of interest only to a minority. [4] Instead, Hugh McLeod has argued that sport has occupied the social space previously occupied by religion:

The belief held by governments and many parents that sport can make you a better person has meant that sport frequently takes over the role formerly performed by the churches of seeking to produce mature adults and good citizens. [5]

He highlights Labour's 2022 new sport and physical education strategy as being straight out of the muscular Christian handbook, with phrases such as this by the then Secretary of State for Media, Culture and Sport, Tessa Jowell, *increased public participation could reduce crime and enhance social inclusion.* [6]

Developments in transport and the shortening of the working week contributed to the growth of crowds in football. In Birmingham, engineering firms began to close at 1.00 on a Saturday from around 1853. This was one of the key reasons why football developed here early. For example, workers would have left the old gas works behind Villa Park and those from the HP Sauce factory at Aston Cross likewise. There were also several other factories nearby, such as Norton Motors, Hercules Cycle and Motor Company and Dunlop Rubber. [7] It is no coincidence that Aston Villa became a key club in developing professionalism and founding the Football League.

One of the factors that marked a break between football and religion, and that of the elite public schools, was indeed professionalism. As Tony Collins stated, this was a force which was seen by the sporting elite as a direct threat to the principles of muscular Christianity:

Professionalism, they believed, would inevitably lead to corruption of sport's ideals by gambling and match-fixing. They feared that professionalism would undermine the structure of football and allow professional players – by which it was understood to mean- working class athletes- to dominate the sport.[8]

Some sports, such as Athletics, had even banned working-class athletes. The Amateur Athletics Club, when it was founded in 1866, listed these qualifications for those who wanted to compete: *Any person who has never competed in an open competition, or for public money, or for admission money, or with professionals for a prize, public or admission money, and who has never, at any period of his life, taught or assisted in the pursuit of athletics as a means of livelihood, or is a mechanic, artisan, or labourer.*[9]

There were concerns that winning at all costs would undermine the values of gentlemen players and inevitably lead to violence. There were also worries that the spectators would revert to the gambling so prevalent in pre-muscular Christian sports.[10] But the fundamental concern was over the loss of amateur status. For Martin Johnes:

..amateurism involved playing the game for its own sake rather than winning, a disdain for gambling and an adherence to fair play, disciplinary codes and winning with grace but losing without candour. Above all, amateurism was about social position. To be an amateur in Victorian and Edwardian Britain was not to need to be paid to play.[11] Johnes is hinting at the class divisions which were to be crystal clear in the split of Rugby in 1895. Working-class sport was a product of the harshness of life in working-class communities, who took up middle-class sports but wanted to play and watch in their own ways.[12]

For Collins, it was the development of cup competitions in the 1870s that first brought money into the game of football. The defeating of local rivals and the winning of cups now had a wider social importance, leading to clubs seeking out players from other areas who could improve their chances.[13] One of the key sources of supply to the northern clubs that were starting to adopt aspects of professionalism was Scotland, particularly Glasgow, which had developed a football culture well before the north of England. The intensity of this culture created a wealth of skillful players who would begin to migrate south in search of higher living standards.

The first wave happened in 1878 when Glasgow Partick FC travelled south to play Darwen in the heart of the Lancashire cotton district. A few months later, two of the players, Fergus Suter and James Love, joined Darwen. Many suspected that they were being paid, and these suspicions were reinforced when Suter was subsequently transferred to Blackburn Rovers. Suter had strong personal reasons for turning professional. He wanted to escape his abusive father and earn an income so that his mother and sisters could also live separately from him. Suter ended up with three FA Cup winners' medals, but his career was petering out when the Football League was created, and he only played one league game.[14] Suter and Love forged a path that would be followed by thousands of other Scottish footballers. This was shown in 1884 when the Scottish FA wrote to fifty-eight Scottish players then playing for English clubs to inform them that they were no longer eligible to play for Scotland as they were considered to be professionals. [15]

In England, this had already led in 1882 to the FA passing a resolution to ban clubs from paying players anything above expenses. This was after a dispute between the FA and Bolton Wanderers, who had unofficially offered professional terms to Scottish players known as the *Scottish Professors*.[16]

Putative professional clubs, such as Preston North End, started to get around this by employing players in the businesses owned by the directors. This was either on a real or made-up basis known as *shamateurism*. This led to suspensions of both Preston and Burnley. It is noteworthy that the FA official investigating this case was Nicholas Lane Jackson. He had set up Corinthian FC in 1882, a club so committed to the principles of amateurism and fair play that they refused to play for cups or prizes and allowed opposing teams to score when they were awarded penalties.[17]

Eventually, in late 1884, seventeen northern clubs formed their own rival British Football Association. A further meeting a week later in Manchester, supported by the Birmingham FA, attracted seventy delegates representing thirty-seven clubs. Eventually, after putting up much resistance, in July 1885, the FA finally accepted professionalism under strict controls such as players being registered with the FA, not being allowed to leave their clubs without permission, and being subject to local residential qualifications if playing in the FA Cup. However, even the FA Cup became out of the reach of amateur clubs and in 1885 Queens Park became the last one to appear in an FA Cup Final when they were beaten 2-0 by Blackburn Rovers. [18]

One of the first clubs to take advantage of the new professionalism was Sunderland. Their mine-owning benefactor, Samuel Tysak, taking advantage of being so close to the border, scouted Scotland for talent, often pretending to be a priest. His team of professional recruits became so dependent on Scotland that, in the 1895 World Championship, the entire team was Scottish.[19] Despite this apparent move away from Christianity, one of the club's early players, Arthur Bridgett 1902-24, refused to play on religious holidays.[20]

Another subsequent team to follow suit was Preston North End. They became the first team to win the League and FA Cup double in 1889, with a majority of their team being Scottish. They became known as *the Invincibles* as they went undefeated in both competitions.[21]

Unlike in football, professionalism in Rugby led to a major split in the game. However, the regional split whereby most northern clubs became professional and went on to found Rugby League had echoes of the amateur/professional divide in football. At the 1886 annual general meeting of the Rugby Football Union, a decision was taken to outlaw payments to players. There is little doubt that this decision was heavily influenced by the previous year's decision of the FA to accept professionalism. In fact, one of the men had voted for the FA's decision. N.L. Jackson had apparently changed his mind and started to advocate pure amateurism on the committee of the RFU.

However, these pressures were resisted in the north and, in 1889, Wakefield Trinity, inspired by the success of the inaugural Football League, called for the formation of a Yorkshire Football League to ensure the maintenance of high-quality rugby. It was in Yorkshire that the RFU decided to clamp down on professionalism, and between 1887 and 1894, two dozen trials of players and clubs took place. This led to the suspension of John Sutcliffe, an England international who promptly changed to playing football. Also, in 1893, the RFU outlawed so-called broken payments to cover loss of earnings for players taking time off from work. The decision led to the suspension of several northern clubs, including Salford, Wigan and Huddersfield. This resulted in 1895 with a meeting of twenty-one clubs at Huddersfield, who decided to resign from the RFU and create the Northern Rugby Football Union, which became the Rugby League within a few years.[22]

The rocketing costs that football clubs were experiencing to enter cup competitions were unsustainable. For example, Blackburn Olympic folded in 1889 because they failed to win another cup tie after the legalisation of professionalism. The only way for the other clubs to avoid the same fate was to develop a more regular income. For some time, cricket had developed an unofficial County championship. As a result, in 1888, the Aston Villa director William McGregor proposed the formation of a league. The creation of the Football League acted as an alternative source of power to the FA and watered down the influence of amateur gentlemen's players. It was significant that a whole series of business criteria were set down as qualifying conditions for the new league, such as proving you could muster a good crowd.[23] The latter was a crucial factor in why Everton, as opposed to then more successful Bootle FC, were admitted to the inaugural Football League. For the first nine seasons of the Football League, they had the highest crowds of any club.[24] They even gained access to the league over more established clubs from other areas like Darwen, Nottingham Forest and Sheffield Wednesday.[25]

One immediate by-product of professionalism was the growth of transfer fees. It has been claimed that the first time that money changed hands between clubs for a professional player was the £100 that Aston Villa paid Preston North End in 1888 for Archie Goodall, whose brother John would help

Villa out of the FA Cup a few months later by when he scored in Preston's 3-1 defeat of them.[26] A few years later, the £400 that Everton paid Blackburn Rovers for striker Jack Southworth, who went on to score 36 goals for his new club in the 1893-94 season, led to new regulations of the transfer market. The Football League then introduced a new rule, which still underpins the transfer system today, requiring players seeking a transfer to obtain permission from their original club. Once signed by a new club, they were obliged to remain there for as long as the club wanted them.

In 1904, Sunderland paid Sheffield United a new record fee of £520 for Alf Common. He subsequently became the first £1000 transfer when he was signed by Middlesbrough in 1905. Despite attempts by the Football League to set limits on the transfer market, the clubs always found ways around them. After World War One, Bolton Wanderers paid £3500 for striker David Jack from Plymouth Argyle; he went on to score the first goal in a Wembley FA Cup Final in 1923 when Bolton beat West Ham 2-0. Five years later, he again became the highest transfer when he was signed by Arsenal for a fee of £10,890. After World War II, the first £20,000 player was Tommy Lawton, who was transferred between Everton and Third Division Notts County.[27]

It was after George Eastham's court case against Newcastle United in 1963, which abolished the retain-and-transfer system, that fees began to significantly increase.[28] Another factor fueling the growth in fees was transfers with foreign clubs, who didn't have the same transfer system. When Denis Law became the first £100,000 transfer from Torino to Manchester United in 1961, it brought another factor into play. Trevor Francis became the first £1 million transfer in 1979 when he moved from Birmingham City to Nottingham Forest, and this has recently culminated in the British record again being broken with the £105 million that Arsenal paid for the West Ham midfielder Declan Rice in 2023.[29] In the same year, a record £7.6 billion was spent on international transfers globally, with English spending the most at £2.3 billion. It marked an incredible 48.1% increase since 2022. A significant pattern for the future was the country second on the list, Saudi Arabia, which spent £765 million.[30]

Professionalism has also led to spiralling wage bills. The first club registered as professional was Blackburn Rovers in 1885-86. During the whole of that season, they spent £615 on wages. By 1888, Nick Ross was reported as receiving £10 per month after his transfer from Preston North End to Everton. By the 1890s, leading clubs like Sunderland, Aston Villa and Newcastle United were paying £5 a week to their best players. A minority of players were reputedly earning £10 per week. All this led to the first proposal by Derby County in 1893 to limit wages to £4 per week. Although this was rejected initially, in 1901, the FA passed this proposal at its AGM. They also voted to ban match bonuses. To compensate players, they introduced a benefit after five years of service to a club. The proposals were to encourage players to stay at clubs and to curb the power of the wealthier clubs. However, top players were against the proposals even though £4 per week was twice what a skilled craftsman earned. They formed a Trade Union, the Association Football Players Union, in 1907. However, the FA outlawed it in 1909, although most players resigned, those at Manchester United and Sunderland remained.

Eventually, after experiencing numerous hardships, they were reinstated in 1909. After the First World War, player wages were capped at £10 per week, but this was reduced to £9 in 1920. The following year, it was reduced to £8 in the season and £6 in the close season, where it remained until 1945. In the 1950s, there were a series of gradual increases, but it was in the 1960s that things changed.[31]

In 1960, the Union, now called The Professional Footballers' Association, decided to campaign against the then-current rate of £20 per week and £17 in the close season. The campaign was led by Fulham striker Jimmy Hill and PFA secretary Cliff Lloyd. A threatened strike led to the FA conceding to the demands of abolishing the maximum wage in 1961.

There was also another back story which may have concentrated the minds of the FA; this was the exodus of top players, like Jimmy Greaves, John Charles and Denis Law, to Italy at a time when there was no maximum wage. The decision had the inevitable consequence of the emergence of an elite group of clubs able to pay the increased salaries and transfer fees.[32]

This really paved the way for the current situation of the top six totally dominating the Premier League and the transfer market. Despite the existence of an elite bunch of superstars that were able to supplement and hugely increase their wages through advertising, like George Best and Kevin Keegan, it wasn't till the advent of the Premier League and satellite TV that wages themselves skyrocketed.

In 1984-85, the average wage of First Division players was £24,934, about two and a half times the average man's salary. In 2009-10, the average Premier League wage was £1.76 million. This marked an increase of forty-six times the average salary then.[33] In 2019, the average salary for a Premier League player had soared to £297,500 per week, whereas the average weekly salary was £717. This is a staggering 415 times less than the Premier League footballer's salary.[34] So, within 30 years, the salary ratio has dramatically increased from two and a half to 415.

Certainly, the salary hike has led to the average Premier League footballer leading a lifestyle totally removed from that of the average fan. Whether that is contrary to Christian values is a matter of opinion, although the experiences of Paul Merson, discussed later, may tend to support Christian fears. However, wage inflation has certainly contributed to the feeling that Premier League football is now unfair and favours the top six. This has led to growing calls for a salary cap, as seen in the calls by Grimsby Chairman Jason Stockwood. He has argued for a cap regulated by the PFA and the Football League, which would allow sustainability and would reduce the influence of agents. It would enable merit-based advancement up the leagues and would allow each club to sign three *marquee* signings per season outside of the cap.[35] It must be said that his proposals don't include the Premier League, which is the main source of the disparities in English football, but are an interesting way to try to resolve the problem.

However, in recent years, the Premier League itself has intervened to try and stop reckless spending. In the 2013-14 season, it introduced its Profit and Sustainability Rules to prevent clubs from spending their way up to the top of the Premier League and reduce the imbalances among the clubs. The current rules state that no club is allowed to lose more than £105 million over three seasons. No clubs were affected until season 2023-24, when both Everton and Nottingham Forest suffered points deductions. In 2024-25, no clubs suffered a similar fate, although Leicester City were let off on a technicality, and, as of writing, no verdict has been reached on the Manchester City case. The latter one will be pivotal as it involved the leader of the 'top six' and involved 115 separate charges.

Recently, the Premier League announced that no clubs breached the rules for the 2023-24 season, leading some commentators to suggest that clubs are finally starting to limit their transfer spending.[36] There are also further Premier League proposals to impose a salary cap from 2025-26. The proposal is to 'anchor' any spending cap to a multiple of the league's lowest earner of prize money and TV revenue, reportedly around 4.5-5. The intention is to reverse the current pattern of the rich getting richer and the gap widening.[37]

It awaits to be seen if any of these proposals are implemented. Historical precedent since the 1960s of wage and transfer inflation leading to a lessening of competition is unpromising. The Premier League needs to avoid the Spanish precedent of 'the big 2' dominating *La Liga*.

As mentioned earlier, the church identified match-fixing as a by-product of professionalism, which would erode the moral ideals of the gentleman amateur. Throughout the history of the professional game, up to the present day, match-fixing has been a significant presence. The first publicised incident in the English game was as early as the final day of the 1904-05 season, when the Manchester City superstar Billy Meredith was accused of offering the Aston Villa captain £10 to throw the match in the final game of the season. It later transpired that Meredith was acting on behalf of manager Tom Maley. This resulted in the club being fined £900 in addition to Meredith's season-long suspension.[38]

In 1915, the match between Manchester United and Liverpool aroused suspicion when Liverpool players apparently showed little effort in their 2-0 defeat. It was subsequently found that a large amount of money had been bet at odds of 7/1 on a 2-0 United victory. An FA investigation was launched and found that players from both sides were involved in the betting. All seven of the guilty players received life bans. Ironically, Meredith, who was playing for Manchester United, wasn't involved.[39]

A more infamous case that was well publicised in the 1960s was the 1964 betting scandal involving two Sheffield Wednesday players betting on their team to lose a game against Ipswich Town in December 1962. They were both subsequently imprisoned and received life bans from the game. They were part of a betting ring involving nine players and one former player, who all received a similar ban. One of the two Wednesday players was England international Tony Kay, who had been transferred to Everton later in December 1962 and would go on to play a starring role in their championship-winning season of 1962-63. His ban was to have devastating consequences for both Everton and England. [40]

In the 1990s, former goalkeeper Bruce Grobbelaar was alleged to have taken £40,000 to make sure that Liverpool lost 3-0 at Newcastle in 1993. *He sued for libel and eventually was awarded £85,000 in 1999.* However, the Sun newspaper appealed, and Grobbelaar's award was reduced to £1 with huge legal costs, which bankrupted him. The judge's summing up would seem to encapsulate Christianity's early fears about match-fixing:

He acted in a way which no decent footballer would act and in a way which could, if not exposed and stamped on, undermine the integrity of a game which earns the loyalty and support of millions.[41]

Grobbelaar still maintains his innocence today, but after the initial allegations, clubs were reluctant to employ him.[42]

Football continues to be rocked by similar scandals, such as the West Ham midfielder Lucas Paqueta's spot-fixing and the Newcastle midfielder Sandro Tonali's betting scandals of 2023.[43] Paqueta was subsequently cleared by an Independent Regulatory Commission in July 2025.

There have been more scandals over the years that I haven't even mentioned, involving players such as Southampton's Matt Le Tissier in the 1990s, to more recently the one with Brentford striker Ivan Toney.

Concerns about match-fixing led in August 2014 to the FA changing its rules to ban players from betting on any football match worldwide or on any football-related matter. This has led to players like Ivan Toney and Sandro Tonali receiving recent bans. The rules also affect managers, club staff and match officials. They also ban them from passing on information to a third party for use in football gambling.[44] In addition to match-fixing, involving players, football clubs themselves have faced numerous corruption allegations over the years, often involving the bribery of referees. Most of them have remained unproven, but some have been thoroughly investigated and have resulted in punishment.

One of the latter was the bribery of the Spanish referee in the 1984 UEFA Semi-Final second leg involving Anderlecht and Nottingham Forest. After winning the first leg 2-0, Forest were defeated 3-0 in Brussels after a dubious penalty decision and a Forest goal being disallowed. It was later discovered that Anderlecht president Constant Vanden Stock had bribed the referee. When this was eventually discovered in 1997, Anderlecht were banned from European competition for a year.[45]

The biggest match-fixing scandal in world football was the *Totonero* scandal in Italy in 1980. It culminated in mass arrests and the relegation of AC Milan and Lazio. The famous Italian striker Paulo Rossi also received a 3-year ban, cut to twelve months to allow him to play a starring role in the 1982 World Cup. Fourteen years later, there was another betting scandal involving Juventus, who were both relegated and had a 30-point deduction imposed. Fiorentina and Lazio were also relegated.[46]

Corruption in football is not limited to the players. Numerous allegations have been made against the football authorities over the years. According to Sugden and Tomlinson, these were particularly directed at FIFA's ex-president Sepp Blatter, who presided over the organisation from 1998-2015. Alan Tomlinson and John Sugden summarised this as: *Blatter reels in the face of accusations of administrative malpractice, financial mismanagement and outright organisational deception and fraud.* [47]

The background to accusations against Blatter started with his election in 1998, with allegations by Farra Ado, the Vice-President of the Confederation of African Football, that he had been offered $100,000 to vote for Blatter. [48] There were also bribery allegations when he was re-elected in 2011.

In 2018, when the World Cup was awarded to Russia, it was controversial due to reports that he had cut an unofficial deal with UEFA head Michel Platini to ensure Europe received

74

the bid.[49] In 2013, a FIFA Ethics Committee investigation into illegal payments to former marketing partner International Sports and Leisure led to Blatter being cleared, but his predecessor, Joao Havelange, being forced to resign from his position as honorary President.[50]

Finally, in 2015, Blatter was suspended for ninety days while investigations were made into payments to Michel Platini, and in 2021, he received a second ban for six years after a probe into bonus payments. To top it all, he was charged by the Swiss authorities for fraud and falsifying documents in connection with improper payments to Platini. Although the charges were subsequently dropped, the image of FIFA as a 'corrupt' body remains under Platini's successor, Gianni Infantino, especially in handing the 2022 World Cup to Qatar with its dubious human rights record. For example, in 2014, the Sunday Times alleged that a Qatari official paid more than £5 million to gain support for hosting the tournament.[51] Infantino oversaw this competition and defended the choice of Qatar from the critics.

All these scandals reveal truths about the professional game that were fully realised by nineteenth-century Christians. There appears to be little that the authorities can do to prevent them from recurring. Prosecutions have done little to stem the flow of corrupt match-fixing, which seems to be an inevitable consequence of the big money flowing into the game. However, early incidents of match-fixing would indicate that professionalism itself has played a role.

As football grew and became increasingly connected to the business world in the early twentieth century, the church gradually disengaged from the game and from sports in general.[52]

One factor was the competition for time between church and sport. By the 1890s, bicycle ownership first challenged the church for Sunday leisure time. By 1914, half of all golf clubs opened on a Sunday, and in the 1924 Olympics, the Scottish sprinter Eric Liddell famously clashed with the Olympic authorities by refusing to race on a Sunday. However, it wasn't until 1960 that the FA lifted its ban on Sunday football, leading to numerous local Sunday leagues being formed. This proved to be a fatal blow for church-based amateur football clubs. In England, the involvement of churches in amateur sports peaked in the 1920s and 30s.

In Bolton in the 1920s, church-based clubs accounted for half of all clubs playing football and cricket. However, there was a gradual decline of church-based sports after the war, which became more rapid in the 1970s and 80s. In 1974, professional matches were allowed on a Sunday for the first time when Cambridge United played Oldham Athletic in the FA Cup.[53]

I personally attended Everton's first Sunday match, in the FA Cup versus West Bromwich Albion, two weeks later. This was held on a Sunday at an earlier kick-off time to reduce the use of electricity during the Miners' strike. A rare recent victory by the church on this issue was secured at the same ground in 2002 when the vicar of the adjacent church of St Luke's, Harry Ross, protested at the proposed kick-off time of 1 pm on a Sunday in an FA Cup game against Crewe Alexandra. He was concerned that the early kickoff time would inconvenience his parishioners attending their morning service. Ross duly won, and the kickoff time was put back to 1.30.[54]

The footballing authorities in Northern Ireland, heavily influenced by Presbyterianism, banned Sunday football until

2008. Sections of the *Sunday Observance Act 1695* are still in force there. However, even after the lifting of the ban, some clubs like Linfield continued to enforce it. But Linfield have had to move with the times due to the pressures of competing in European football, so in 2020 they amended their constitution to allow the team to play on a Sunday only if they had a European game on the previous Sunday.[55] However, a recent vote by the Irish Football Association to abolish the remaining restrictions on Sunday football was defeated at its 2023 AGM by 104-27.[56] This was reinforced the following year when the Northern Ireland League Cup's proposals to waive objections to Sunday playing for the latter stages of the trophy were rejected after an appeal by Loughall FC.[57] Even some of the players have opposed playing on a Sunday. In the 1982 World Cup in Spain, Northern Ireland player and born-again Christian Johnny Jameson refused to play against France as the match was on a Sunday.[58]

Catholic countries had a more relaxed attitude to Sunday football, with Sunday fixtures being instated at a relatively early stage in their footballing history. A relatively recent set of guidance from Pope Francis gives a clue to this attitude. In 2018, he stated that Catholics should feel free to play sports on the Sabbath because it *can help integrate a family with other families in the celebration of Sunday.*[59] It's worth noting that the Gaelic Athletic Association arranged its matches on a Sunday from early in its inception, and when Southern Irish football clubs formed their own association, the Football Association of Ireland, in 1921, they permitted Sunday matches from the start. [60]

Clubs in Muslim countries have also had problems when fixtures clash with religious holidays. The Egyptian team Al-

Ahly requested that their African Champions League fixture against Orlando Pirates be rescheduled to avoid clashing with the Ramadan fasting period.[61] In 2016, clerics in Iran tried to postpone the country's World Cup qualifying match with South Korea due to it clashing with the two holiest days in the Shia Muslim calendar, Tasua and Ashura.[62]

Another area of concern over the commercialisation of football for the church was gambling. While unlike other vices like adultery, theft and drunkenness, there are no clear admonitions against gambling in the Bible, there are several indirect criticisms. For example, in 1 Timothy, it warns that *those who want to get rich fall into temptation and a trap into many foolish and harmful desires that plunge people into ruin and destruction. For the love of money is a root of all kinds of evil.*[63]

So, for many clergymen, gambling was seen as the embodiment of all that was wrong with the commercialisation of sport. It was a way of getting money without working for it, and it led to crime. According to Congregationalist preacher R.F. Horton, gambling was wrong in itself, whereas alcohol wasn't wrong if taken in moderation. The contrast with the original muscular Christian ideals of courage, presence of mind and self-reliance couldn't be stronger.[64]

It's worth stating that the Catholic church has always had a more nuanced attitude to gambling, as illustrated by the catechism, no 2404, which states:

Games of chance …are not in themselves contrary to justice. They become morally unacceptable when they deprive (people) of what is necessary to provide for (their) needs and those of others.[65]

The nonconformist churches, which disproportionately influenced the early FA, had a more literal interpretation of the

Bible. They were more likely to see gambling as breaching the first, second, eighth and tenth commandments.[66]

The FA had excluded gambling in football at an early stage, following the Betting Houses Act 1853, which made off-course horse racing betting illegal.[67] However, it was powerless to act against the pools' companies. Although the first company, Littlewoods, wasn't established until 1923, there were smaller equivalents in the late nineteenth century. For example, in 1887, the *Cricket and Football Field* newspaper offered a prize of one guinea to any reader who predicted the results of four of next week's football matches.[68] The Football Association became concerned about gambling by spectators and, in 1892, required clubs to take steps to ban it. In 1897, it required clubs to put up bills on football grounds to clearly point out the illegality of gambling within the grounds.[69]

In 1908, it banned any type of gambling connected with football. Five years later, as a reaction to coupon betting, it suspended any football official who was proven to have taken part in coupon betting and to change players' contracts to incorporate a termination clause if they were similarly involved. [70] It's worth noting that the FA's attitude was strongly influenced by Christianity.

The National Anti-Gambling League had been formed in 1890. It saw gambling as being against Christian values and was dominated by Quaker and Non-Conformist religions. A major leader of the movement was Charles Sutcliffe, a key member of the National Football League Committee and a devout and strict Methodist. He eventually became Chairman of the Football League in 1935. He became a forceful figure in acting against the football pools.[71]

Football figures played a key part in the passing of the Ready Money Betting Act 1920, which tried to outlaw coupon betting in football. The FA were the main lobbying group for the Act, and, in parliament, it was supported by the Arsenal Chairman, Sir Henry Norris.[72]

In 1923, John Moores, the future Chairman of Everton, and two friends launched Littlewoods from a Liverpool office after hearing about a Birmingham man launching a similar project. After initial difficulties, the two friends pulled out, but by 1930, Moores became a millionaire.[73]

The reaction of the football authorities to the pools was predictable; in 1920, the Chairman of the FA, J. Charles Clegg said – *if betting gets hold of football, the game is done for.*[74] In 1929, the inevitable happened, Moores was prosecuted under the Ready Money Betting Act 1920. However, he was let off on a technicality as he required payment in postal orders, not cash. Paradoxically, the collapse of the case gave Moores the publicity to expand the business.

In 1936, the new Chairman of the Football League, Charles Sutcliffe, tried to issue a knock-out blow to the pools by initiating a so-called 'pools war.' Their main weapon in this campaign was their copyright ownership of the fixture list. They issued a new fixture list, which would be withheld until two days before the fixtures. However, due to the logistics of playing the matches, they had to tell the clubs, and this eventually slipped out to the pools' companies. After facing a rebellion by 36 of the 44 Football League members, the league was forced to climb down.

Also, in 1936, a Private Members' Bill to outlaw the Football Pools supported by the MP R.J. Russell, who claimed to have the support of Sir Frederick Wall of the FA and of the

Scottish and Welsh FAs, was crushingly defeated by 287-24. [75] The historian Dave Russell saw these defeats as considerable ones for the non-conformists, being custodians of Victorian values.[76] It also paved the way for the Football Pools Promoters' Association to expand their business freely, without interference from the football authorities. This process lasted up to the peak in the 1960s and 70s. [77]

The dramatic growth of Littlewoods in the post-war period led to John Moores in 1960 giving up Chairmanship of the pools business and handing it over to his brother Cecil, so he could become a director, and later in the year, Chairman of Everton Football Club. Under his Chairmanship, the club became the wealthiest one in the country and was dubbed *the Mersey Millionaires.* Subsequently, under the twin alternatives of the national Lottery and online gambling, the pools declined.

Today, online football betting is a huge global phenomenon. Mark O'Haire sees two key factors in promoting its growth. Firstly, in 1992, Sky Sports bought the rights to broadcast Premier League matches. This led to placing bets on football matches being accepted by the bookmakers. In the mid-1990s, in-running betting was launched, which allowed punters to bet on a live TV game as it was happening.

Secondly, the enormous growth of the internet at the turn of the century revolutionised betting in many ways, but perhaps the most significant was allowing punters to bet at home and take odds from the vast number of online operators that have subsequently developed. This created an appeal to the younger generation of punters, deterred by the traditional *smoke-filled* rooms of the betting shops, the preserve of middle-aged male punters. Online betting also benefitted from the abolition of the betting tax in 2001. The wider media also began to pick up on this, with stations like Sky Sports and Talk Sport quoting match odds.

Consequently, horse racing has seen its betting market share go down, whereas that of football has hugely increased. [78] At the start of the 2024/25 season, research suggested that betting adverts had almost trebled compared with the previous season. This is despite a new code of conduct being published within the industry to curb marketing during sports events. But the report's co-lead author, Dr. Rafaello Rossi, suggests that this hasn't affected the volume of adverts. [79]

The development of mobile technology has also led to data and analytics being more important tools in football betting. Both punters and bookmakers use detailed statistics and performance data to make more informed decisions. This has led to more complex and strategic betting being developed. Artificial intelligence is likely to revolutionise the business further by analysing vast amounts of data to identify patterns and providing predictive information. These will be adjusted to individual users, resulting in more users. [80]

At first glance, the rise of online football betting seems to sound the final death knell for the predominantly Christian groups that originally voiced concerns about the moral perils of professionalism in football. However, Governments and Sports Authorities have recognised the potential risks associated with unregulated betting and have moved to ensure fair play and consumer protection through establishing frameworks.

For example, in 2005, the UK Gambling Commission was established. It is responsible for licensing and regulating iGaming operators to ensure fair and transparent operations.

Operators are required to set deposit limits, self-exclude and access support for gambling-related issues.[81]

Within the game, the most obvious step taken recently to control online football gambling is the decision taken by the Premier League in 2023 to phase out team shirt sponsorship by gambling companies by the summer of 2026. As it is a voluntary agreement, clubs will still be allowed to promote these companies on their shirt sleeves and pitch-side advertising hoardings. At the time, eight Premier League clubs, including Everton, had betting companies as front shirt sponsors, and two more had betting-related sleeve adverts. [82]

The ban stems from the sharp increase in gambling addiction across the UK. In 2023, the UK Gambling Commission published figures suggesting that as many as 2.5% of UK adults may be suffering from a gambling problem.[83]

More widely known to football fans are the well-publicised cases of footballers who end up with gambling addictions. Former England goalkeeper Peter Shilton is reported to have lost more than £50,000 over a 45-year period, admitting that his losses increased significantly with the advent of online gambling.[84]

In recent years, the best publicised case has involved pundit and ex-player Paul Merson. In his 2021 memoir *Hooked,* he calculates that he has lost over £7 million during his playing career and gambled away his £750,000 PFA pension when offered it as a lump sum when he retired.[85] He is now blocked from all betting companies, and all his considerable income gets paid straight into the bank account of his third wife, so he doesn't blow it on gambling.

Football's schizophrenic relationship with gambling can be illustrated with my own club, Everton. In 2020, the club's Chief Executive, Denise Barrett-Baxendale, announced the end of its shirt sponsorship deal with online gambling company SportPesa. Keen to promote a socially responsible image, she confirmed it would be replaced by a partnership with car hire firm Cazoo, which also pledged to donate £50,000 annually to the club's pioneering initiative, *Everton in the Community.*[86]

However, within two years, Cazoo had been replaced with the US online betting company *Stake*. The financial attractions for a club struggling to compete with the burgeoning wealth of the top six Premier League clubs were obvious. In 2022, the club was further affected by the Russian invasion of Ukraine, which brought an end to its £12 million-a-year training ground sponsorship and the £30 million pledged for naming rights of the new stadium. It's the largest front-of-shirt deal in the club's history, worth more than £10 million per year. [87]

However, at the time of writing, there is a big question mark about the sustainability of the *Stake* deal. In February 2025, it was announced that *Stake* was giving up its licence in the UK. The Gambling Commission will write to Everton and two other clubs, Nottingham Forest and Leicester City, who also have deals with unlicensed betting companies in the UK, warning them of their responsibilities to ensure that these companies can't be accessed in the UK.[88]

Online football gambling is an area that football authorities have struggled to control. It is a clear sign of the worries nineteenth-century Christianity had for the game when it turned professional.

Religion and football continue to be a controversial issue with many Brazilian stars who adhere to the Pentecostal faith, such as Kaka and Lucio, openly displaying religious symbols on their t-shirts, which appear to be contrary to FIFA's ban on religious or political slogans on players' attire.

The response of FIFA was merely to issue the Brazilian FA with a warning letter.[89] This continues to be an issue in English football, with the Crystal Palace defender Marc Guehi not being prosecuted over wearing armbands with religious messages like *I love Jesus and Jesus Loves You*. The FA has a similar ban to FIFA's, and they are in a particularly difficult position as they are among the eight voters on the 138-year-old panel of the International Football Association Board.[90]

The Guehi case was particularly significant as the armbands were part of the Premier League's inclusion issue of supporting the Rainbow Laces campaign against gay discrimination. Guehi was merely reminded of the FA's rules on the issue of religious slogans.[91] The Chelsea Ukrainian player Mykhailo Mudryk has found a novel way of avoiding any charges by having his Christian slogans tattooed over his body, including one saying *Only Jesus* clearly displayed on his neck.[92] The lack of effective action over these cases by the football authorities shows that their attempts to distance themselves from religion may be failing; this was amply illustrated with the rather ritualistic way that the FA merely wrote to Cody Gakpo who, after scoring a goal in Liverpool's Premier league clincher against Tottenham Hotspur, lifted his shirt to reveal the message *I belong to Jesus* on his vest underneath.[93] They can also be justified in being hypocritical in not prosecuting these Christian players, whereas, in 2013, the Ghanaian player Mubarak Wakaso received a one-match ban for revealing the slogan *Allah is Great* on his t-shirt.[94]

One successful case against a football club displaying Christian symbols on their kit was paradoxically in Birmingham, Alabama, in the heart of the American *Bible Belt*. The indoor team, *The Steeldogs,* wore jerseys with books of the Old Testament and verse numbers printed on the backs of their warm-up shirts as part of the Faith Nights programme. However, despite these events leading to a fifteen per cent increase in attendance, after being threatened with a $25,000 fine by their league, they withdrew the shirts.[95]

Another apparently successful American case of a clampdown against a Christian player expressing her views was the non-inclusion in the US women's World Cup squad in 2018 of full-back Jaelene Hinkle. This was after she refused to wear a Gay Pride t-shirt as it went against her Christian beliefs. She had also previously refused to play for the team after wearing jerseys with rainbow-coloured numbers during Gay Pride week.[96]

When the Brazilian international Neymar played for Paris St Germain, there was allegedly a $500,000 per week clause in his contract to stop him getting involved in *political or religious propaganda* that may tarnish the image of the club. However, he regularly praised God on his social media platforms. He had previously worn a headband, after winning the Champions League with Barcelona, with *100% Jesus* written on it.[97]

The French sportswriter Nicolas Vilas has concluded that the footballing authorities may be wasting their breath in trying to keep religion and football entirely separate.[98]

Several ex-professional footballers have also turned to religion after leaving the game. The first case in my lifetime to attract public attention was that of Wolverhampton Wanderers midfielder Peter Knowles, who had been likened to George Best. However, after an encounter with two Jehovah's Witnesses while on loan to Kansas Spurs in America, he chose to retire from football at the age of 23. [99]

More recently, in 2008, former Chelsea player Mateja Kežman announced his desire to become a monk. Similarly, Brazilian star Kaká expressed an ambition to become a preacher, whilst Argentine goalkeeper Carlos Roa retired at the age of 20 to devote himself to life as a Seventh-day Adventist preacher.[100] The ex-Chelsea player Gavin Peacock started attending his local Methodist church at 18, and after he retired, he became a preacher at his local church. He then studied Divinity at Ridley Hall, Cambridge, before moving to Canada, where he is now a pastor at the Calvary Grace church in Calgary.[101]

The Dutch team of 2024 contains more openly religious players than ever before, according to Mariecke van den Berg. She has identified 15 of the 26-man squad as such. [102] A recent *Spectator* article even suggested that the rise of Christianity in football was unstoppable. It has christened Christian members of the England squad, comprising of Eze, Saka, Ivan Toney and Guehi, as the *God Squad*. Sam Matthews Boehmer explains this as being tied to the increased professionalism and pressures that the modern game has brought. Christianity may be providing a mental outlet and a moral reference point. A crucial factor also appears to be that all these players are from first, second or third-generation immigrant families whose evangelical, or Pentecostal, churches have bucked the trend of declining attendance.[103]

Selina Stone, who lectures on political theology in London, sees Black Pentecostal churches as the fastest-growing in London. Bukhayo Saka attended the Pentecostal Kingsborough Centre in Uxbridge before moving to be closer to Arsenal's training ground. Selina Stone sees Saka and the current generation of black Christian players as feeling that they have a responsibility to help others.[104] Marcus Rashford's Christian faith is a key factor in his fundraising to feed poor children. As many as four million children are estimated to be fed by charities funded or supported by him.[105] The Crystal Palace defender Maxence Lacroix is a Catholic and carries a Bible in a special case. He cites his faith as giving him inner peace and is helping *Spires*, a charity which supports people experiencing homelessness in South London.[106] With Marc Guehi, he completes a Christian central defensive partnership for Crystal Palace. The academic John Maiden has even gone so far as to state that – *in our celebrity and sports-driven culture. It is probably footballers who offer the most high-profile manifestation of religious practice and belief in British public life.* [107]

Some footballers with strong religious convictions have even resisted promoting club sponsors who appear to go against their religious beliefs. In 2013, the Muslim Senegalese player Papiss Cisse didn't go to the club's pre-season training camp as he was consulting his family about what he should do about wearing shirts emblazoned with *Wonga,* a short-term, high-interest loan firm that would appear to infringe Muslim beliefs opposing interest-based transactions. In 2006, the then Sevilla player Frederic Kanoute refused to wear a shirt promoting the gambling company *888*.[108] Kanoute also demonstrated his strong Muslim convictions the following year when he paid $700,000 of his own money, almost a year's salary, on buying his own mosque, to be used by the local Muslim population in Seville, which would have been forced to close otherwise. Kanoute converted to Islam in 1997.[109] Another contemporary example of a committed Muslim player is Bournemouth's Dango Ouattara. He prays five times a day, including before and after matches. He says his faith helps him remain humble and reflect on both the team's successes and its shortcomings. [110]

In Malaysia, there have been calls for Muslim players to avoid wearing shirts bearing badges with crosses, such as those of Brazil or Barcelona. However, a more successful example was in 2012 when Real Madrid dropped crosses on top of their club crest crown, which appeared on their promotional materials when they became involved in a partnership to build a $1 billion sports resort in the United Arab Emirates.[111] There is also a similar commercial view that many of the prominent Muslim footballers apparently attracted to play in Saudi Arabia by massive salaries, may also be attracted to playing in a Muslim country. There have been several recent examples, such as Real Madrid's Karim Benzema, Chelsea's N'Golo Kanté, Lens' Seko Fofana, Lyon's Moussa Dembele and Manchester City's Riyad Mahrez. However, Benzema has gone on record stating that he went *because I am Muslim and it's a Muslim country.*[112]

The current Church of England is aware that all these examples of religious commitment show the potential football still has to spread the word of God and sees its recent *National Sport and Wellbeing Project* as more explicitly evangelistic than Victorian muscular Christianity with its emphasis on using church premises for sport, setting up new sports clubs and after-school clubs and holiday camps.[113]

It also needs to be noted that most top-flight clubs now have community programmes whose values are strongly influenced by Christianity. One of the oldest is *Everton in the Community*, set up in 1988. Situated in one of the poorest areas in the country it's mission statement could fit in neatly to the values of nineteenth century Christian Socialists – *Our vision is for a world where everyone has access to the support, they need to be the best they can be, regardless of who they are, where they live or the challenges they meet.* [114]

The scheme currently has 120+ full-time staff and 160+ volunteers. It offers more than fifty programmes covering social issues such as health, employability, anti-social behaviour, crime, education, dementia, poverty, youth engagement, youth justice and disability. [115]

In 2015, the Sports Journalist Henry Winter said – *All Premier League clubs are involved in community work, but few do it as well as* Everton. [116]

Over the three-year broadcast deal 2022-2024, the Premier League has invested £400 million in funding development of facilities and community and education projects.[117]

Today, all Premier League clubs have their own charitable foundations that work closely with their own communities. One example is the *Palace for Life Foundation*, which works with an annual budget of three million euros. Its Chief Executive, Mike Summers, explains how it works – *We operate in schools, football communities, and the disability sector, addressing issues such as mental health, particularly among 16-24-year-olds.*[118]

90

In 2020, all twenty Premier League clubs had programmes to help their communities during lockdown. These ranged from donating larger amounts of food to FareShare schemes in Birmingham by Aston Villa to Liverpool's £40,000 donation to the St Andrews foodbank and a social isolation initiative contacting the vulnerable by telephone. [119]

All these initiatives have been seen by Irish writer Gerald Gallagher, who works with the *Association of Leaders of Missionaries and Religious of Ireland,* as showing that sport has the capacity to bring people together, crossing barriers, uniting spectators and participants, and, for some observers, replacing the religious experience. As such, it can potentially play a great role in energising and supporting the church in Ireland.[120]

European football authorities are becoming more sensitive to the religious convictions of Muslim players. Football is certainly becoming more sympathetic to Ramadan as in the 2023-24 season Liverpool adjusted their training times during the fast, and the Premier League has started to allow captains to request a break for their players to break their fast during evening games.[121]

In Belgium, the Netherlands, Australia and England, short breaks are allowed in matches during Ramadan. However, the French authorities oppose breaks due to the French state's support of secularism and religious neutrality.[122] The then Tottenham Hotspur forward Arnaut Danjuma claimed in 2023 that fasting during Ramadan made him stronger and perform better on the pitch, leading to him scoring more goals.[123] English football's greater sympathy to the needs of Muslim players was amply illustrated in 2019 when the Premier League replaced bottles of champagne for its player of the month award and replaced them with trophies after Manchester City's

Muslim player Yaya Toure started winning them on a regular basis.[124] Clubs are increasingly also offering prayer facilities for Muslim fans. Seven offer match-day prayer facilities, and the recent Tottenham Hotspur stadium was built to incorporate multi-faith prayer rooms. Similar facilities are also available at both Wembley Stadium and the England training ground, St. George's Park.[125]

The growth of professionalism and gambling in football would tend to indicate that football has fully disengaged with religion, but the failure of both FIFA and the FA to fully implement their ban on religious slogans on players' attire would tend to suggest otherwise. There is also the difficult issue of homosexuality, with several Christian players apparently being able to flaunt their opposition to Premier League initiatives such as supporting the Rainbow Laces campaign. The apparent increasing numbers of footballers turning to religion also suggest that the game isn't a spiritual vacuum of inflated wages and gambling addictions, as is the dramatic increase in clubs' community programmes. The previously quoted examples of Brazilian Pentecostal players were also united with the Catholic players and manager in the 2014 World Cup finals campaign through commonly repeating the Lord's Prayer before matches and visiting a chapel in the grounds of their hotel in Fortaleza.[126] The Moroccan team in the 2022 World Cup recited the first chapter of the Quran before their penalty shootout.[127] In many parts of Africa, the religious practices of the traditional African religion of Juju continue to affect football. For example, many players chew powder before matches to bring strength.[128]

The failure of the football authorities to outlaw match-fixing and the growth of gambling addictions linked to football betting would tend to endorse early worries by church leaders on professionalism in football. However, the persistence of religious faith among both players and fans would indicate that religion will always have an influence over football. In at least one case, the Liverpool Egyptian international Mohamed Salah has succeeded in converting an anti-Islamic Notts Forest fan to Islam. Ben Bird turned from having a hatred of Muslims to becoming one while doing a dissertation on Mohamed Salah whilst at university. [129]

The next chapter examines the role of religion in the formation of Everton Football Club and how football spread to the city of Liverpool in the late nineteenth century.

CHAPTER 5

THE SPREAD OF FOOTBALL IN LATE NINETEENTH-CENTURY LIVERPOOL

On the face of it, Liverpool in the late nineteenth century was not a promising location for churches to inspire the growth of sporting organisations:

Only 19.9% of Liverpool's half million population were churchgoers in 1881, which compared to 40% in Bristol, and 24% in Nottingham, Burnley and Bolton. [1]

There was also a significantly lower than average number of Oxbridge-educated clergy in the city, so it was unusual in the 1870s for five Cambridge-educated Anglican curates to settle in the area. Cambridge was in the middle of an evangelical reawakening at the time, and all five were imbued with the values of muscular Christianity and Christian Socialism. Thomas Preston believes that all five saw Liverpool as a particular challenge, and they may have had the intention of using football as a religious vehicle from the start. They had all attended St. John's College in the 1870s, which had played a significant role in the evolution of Cambridge's football rules, which, in turn, were influential in the drawing up of the first Football Association code.[2] This could be a key reason why they were keen to promote football in their parishes.

At the same time, Methodism in the city had been growing in the early nineteenth century. It had already set up two city chapels in the late eighteenth century and, in 1811, the

Brunswick Chapel was opened in Moss Street. Day schools were built in Erskine Street in 1862. In 1876, the first Central Mission in Methodism was established at the old Pitt Street chapel.[3]

In 1797, Methodism suffered a major split when Alexander Kilham and William Thom founded the Methodist New Connexion, which wanted equal rights for Ministers and the Laity. It later became known for its missionary work in China and played a similar role in many northern cities.[4] Into this church in Liverpool in the 1870s would enter Ben Swift Chambers. He was born into a much humbler family than the five Cambridge-educated Anglican curates. This was in a weaver's cottage near Huddersfield in 1845. Initially, he became an apprentice engraver and was about to be offered a partnership in the business when he felt a calling to be a Methodist minister. Eventually, he joined the New Connexion chapel of St Domingo's in the Everton district of Liverpool in 1871; he was appointed circuit superintendent and minister in 1877. There, he became a promoter of the Band of Hope movement, which was a temperance movement for working-class youngsters. [5]

When St Domingo's Chapel was first opened in 1871, it wasn't necessarily due to the success of the Methodist New Connexion in Liverpool, as it replaced three chapels that had been closed due to falling attendances. [6]

The first of the Cambridge-educated Anglican curates to arrive in the Liverpool region was 25-year-old Alfred Keely. In 1877, he was appointed curate in the dockland's parish of St. John's in Bootle. However, it wasn't until two years later that club fixtures were started. This wasn't due to a church influence but from that of an official from the Shropshire

Union and Canal Company, Robert Lythgoe. He established a club in Birkenhead not long after he arrived in 1879. The first match between St John's and the Birkenhead team was in November 1879. Such was the esteem held in the Northwest for Lythgoe that in 1880, he even arranged a match with Blackburn Olympic, who famously became the first northern team to win the FA Cup in 1883 when they beat Old Etonians. Lythgoe borrowed several St. John's players for the match, including Keely's two brothers. [7]

In the Everton district of Liverpool, another Cambridge-educated curate, Edward Moseley, became curate at St. Saviour's in 1878 after the parish church of St. George's was split into four due to the rising population in the district. The following year, Moseley and the other parish curates formed a football team called the Everton United Football Club. They played in nearby Stanley Park but were not of the same standard as the Bootle and Birkenhead teams. [8]

It's at this point of the story that accounts start to differ. The traditional view holds that Everton FC emerged firstly from a cricket team and subsequently from the football club established at St Domingo's Methodist New Connexion chapel in 1878 by the newly appointed minister, Ben Swift Chambers. This interpretation was originally put forward by Everton FC's first historian, Thomas Keates, in his seminal 1929 work–History of the Everton Football Club. [9]

Keates was a self-made Coal merchant who played a prominent role in the Anfield community where he lived. By 1890, he acquired shares in the new Everton Football Club. In 1894, he was one of a group of majority rebel shareholders who broke away from the club under the chairmanship of John Houlding and would form a separate Everton club to be based at Goodison Park. In 1897, Keates became a director of this club.[10]

After leaving the board, he became preoccupied with jotting down his recollections of the early days of the club, which would form the basis of his later book, published in the year following his death. This becomes the first documented evidence that St Domingo's chapel was the originator of Everton Football Club.

For Thomas Preston, Thomas Keates' account is false. He claims that there is no historical evidence of this link:

Keates' history of the club tells us that Everton FC derived from the St. Domingo's New Connection Methodist Church FC, which itself was an offshoot of the latter's cricket club. Keates also claims that St. Domingo's played several teams in Stanley Park, including St.Mary's (Kirkdale), and three other church teams from Everton, the United Church, St.Peter's, and St. Benedict's. However, whilst matches involving the latter teams were frequently reported in the contemporary press, not a single mention of St. Domingo's has been found in Liverpool newspapers of the period. Moreover, no football was reported in the local press in the Liverpool district during 1878-79, the only year of St. Domingo's alleged existence. [11]

I have to say that my own research has found evidence of such articles. For example, on 20th October 1879, *the Liverpool Daily Courier* reported that St Domingo beat Everton United Reform Church Club 1-0. Peter Lupson even claims that as St Domingo became more adept at football, they attracted the better players from Everton United, St. Benedict's and St. Peter's.[12] Thomas Keates asserted that the presence of numerous players from other churches led, in 1879, to the adoption of the name Everton FC, after the district in which St Domingo's was situated.[13]

Also, a 1893 handbook in the David France Everton collection on the history of the club refers specifically to members of the St. Domingo's Cricket Club forming a football section:

In the following year,1879, the club was properly organised under the name of St. Domingo Football Club. Matches were played against St. Mary's, St. Peter's, Everton United Church and, Bootle St. John's ... [14]

Thomas Keates also documented that St. Domingo's played these other church teams. [15]

Another crucial piece of evidence supporting the role of St Domingo's in creating Everton FC comes from Norman Swain's short history of St. Domingo's Church. In going through church records, he finds that soccer was included within the church activities in 1878, with a team being formed in that year, which changed its name to Everton FC the following year. The history also shows that George Mahon, the church organist, became one of the leaders of the breakaway group, which moved to Goodison Park in 1892, and that one-time choirmaster and St. Domingo trustee Will Cuff became a director of the club from 1895 to 1949. [16]

There also exists a photograph of the St. Domingo Football Club Management Committee, which changed the club name to Everton FC during a meeting at the Queen's Head pub in November 1879. Its Secretary, John W. Clarke, was the son of the pub's landlord. The name change was due to the large growth of crowds, and it was significant that the name Everton was selected, as the St. Domingo church was in the district of Everton. [17]

However, Preston believes that Thomas Keates, as one of the leaders of the rebel board members who split from Chairman John Houlding in 1892, wanted to discredit the role of the brewer John Houlding in forming the club. Preston believes that Houlding was the key figure in creating Everton Football Club from as early as December 1879. He was also on the Lay vestry committee of St. Saviour's church, which was a key part of the Everton United Football Club. When Everton FC split in 1892, Preston sees the new Connexion members on the board as having an interest in discrediting Houlding and promoting St. Domingo's in the formation of the club. Therefore, he sees them promoting *the St. Domingo Myth*. So, who were these people? According to Preston the three leaders of the rebellion were – George Mahon, Dr. James Baxter and W. R. Clayton. [18]

We can immediately dismiss Dr Baxter as one of those referred to, as he was a Catholic. He did much to foster the non-sectarian background of the club as he worked closely with the other mainly Nonconformist members of the board and even attended the funeral of John Houlding. This was an amazing gesture of reconciliation as Houlding was a prominent member of the Orange Order. [19]

Admittedly, George Mahon did have Nonconformist links. This does seem to be mainly through attendance at the Wesleyan Chapel in Great Homer Street.[20] However, David Kennedy + Michael Collins have found evidence that both he, and Will Cuff, a future Chairman of the club, were laymen at the New Connexion chapel of St. Domingo's.[21] WR Clayton just seems to have generally Liberal political affiliations.

Certainly, there were prominent members of St. Domingo's among the rebels. However, there appears to be no documentary evidence of a 'conspiracy' to promote the *St. Domingo Myth*. I tend to agree with David Kennedy that the rebellion was mainly influenced by the political divide between Conservatives, as represented by John Houlding and his allies, and Liberals such as Mahon and Baxter.[22]

I have no reason to contest Thomas Keates' view that John Houlding's involvement in Everton FC was mainly due to their original ground being opposite the 'Stanley House' residence of Houlding.[23] As a shrewd businessman and aspiring politician, his motivations for involvement weren't predominantly religious.

A particular factor in magnifying the split was the growing importance of the temperance issue in the 1880s within the Liberal Party. This culminated in 1891 with the Newcastle programme of 1891, a year before the split. This incorporated a proposal to grant voters a vote on the granting of local liquor licenses. This was particularly relevant in Liverpool, which had 23 of the 83 temperance organisations represented at the 1884 National Temperance Congress. One direct consequence of this policy was to reinforce the traditionally close links between the brewing industry and the Conservative Party. At the same time, the growth of the city of Liverpool, together with the 1867 enfranchisement of large sections of the urban working class, was threatening the dominance over local politics that the Conservatives had enjoyed since the 1850s. The district of Everton was a particular focus for this division with the existence of two prominent temperance lodges, *the Good Templar* and Band *of Hope*. Its council seat was also being contested by a brewery-owning Conservative, John Houlding, a contest he would eventually win. David Kennedy and

Michael Collins summarised the background factors in the split as:

The factional struggle for control of the club became deeply intertwined with the wider moral social concerns being expressed in the political sphere and control of the club became a contested prize in the moral and political dispute over drink. [24]

At the end of the day, the rebel leaders were Liberals and Houlding, and his main supporters were Conservatives. This represented a far clearer division than any based on religion.

CONCLUSION

The main force behind the development of Association football in the nineteenth century was that of muscular Christianity. In England, this philosophy became embedded in the beliefs of both Anglican and Nonconformist churches. In Scotland and Ireland, there was also a parallel development of muscular Catholicism. These beliefs influenced British churches to have a huge impact on the establishment of many early football clubs. In Ireland, they influenced the establishment of the Gaelic Athletics Association, which influenced Irish sports such as Gaelic football and hurling.

The spread of the game abroad was also indirectly influenced by muscular Christianity through English schools in South America and missionary schools in Africa and Asia.

By the end of the nineteenth century, the church was starting to become more distant from the sport. The onset of professionalism led to a whole series of consequences, like the inflation of player salaries and gambling, which appear to have finally eradicated all religious influence from the sport.

However, religion continues to influence the game. Most Football League clubs have chaplains; these weren't present in early football clubs once the church link had been broken. They also have well-funded community programmes with a distinctly Christian-based ethos. There have been a whole range of modern clubs throughout the world formed by different religious groups. Several prominent players also continue to wear religious symbols whilst playing. Footballing authorities, in trying to stamp this out, seem to be fighting a losing battle. Hugh McLeod believes that recent initiatives by the Church of England suggest that it is still very much influenced by Victorian muscular Christian values today. [1]

In view of the relative success of football's global spread, perhaps the words of Joseph writing on the *Nairaland Forum* are a fitting summary of the current relationship between football and religion:

I want to emphasize strongly and passionately that what religion (Christianity and Islam) have failed to do football has done ... that is bringing both Christians and Muslims, as well as Hindus and Buddhists, under one roof to co-exist peacefully. [2]

About the Author

Bob Waterhouse has previously published *Everton: The Fans Born Not Manufactured*, published in 2022, which has sold over 1000 copies. This covers the social and economic background of the fans and how they have evolved since the club's formation in 1878. In 2024, he published *Liverpool FC Ruined My Life: Sixty Years of Supporting Everton*, an autobiographical account of his 60 years supporting Everton. In February 2025, he published *Bramley Moore Dock: From Slavery to Football at the New Home of Everton FC*, a historical account of the history of the stadium site and the city of Liverpool. He has been interviewed on Talk Sport, BBC Radio Merseyside and the Liverpool Echo about his books. He has also done online interviews with fan sites.

Photo Gallery

1. Ben Swift Chambers (Founder of St. Domingo's Football Team)

THE FIGHT

2. Muscular Christianity

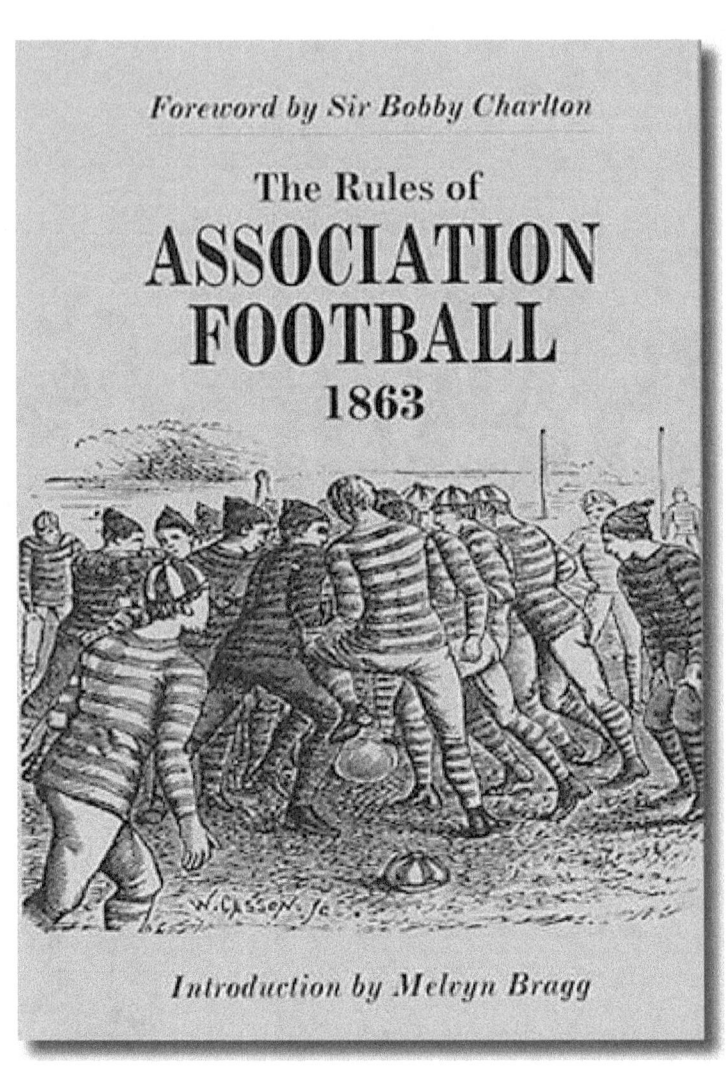

Foreword by Sir Bobby Charlton

The Rules of
ASSOCIATION
FOOTBALL
1863

Introduction by Melvyn Bragg

3. Rules of the FA

4. Early Photograph of Villa Park

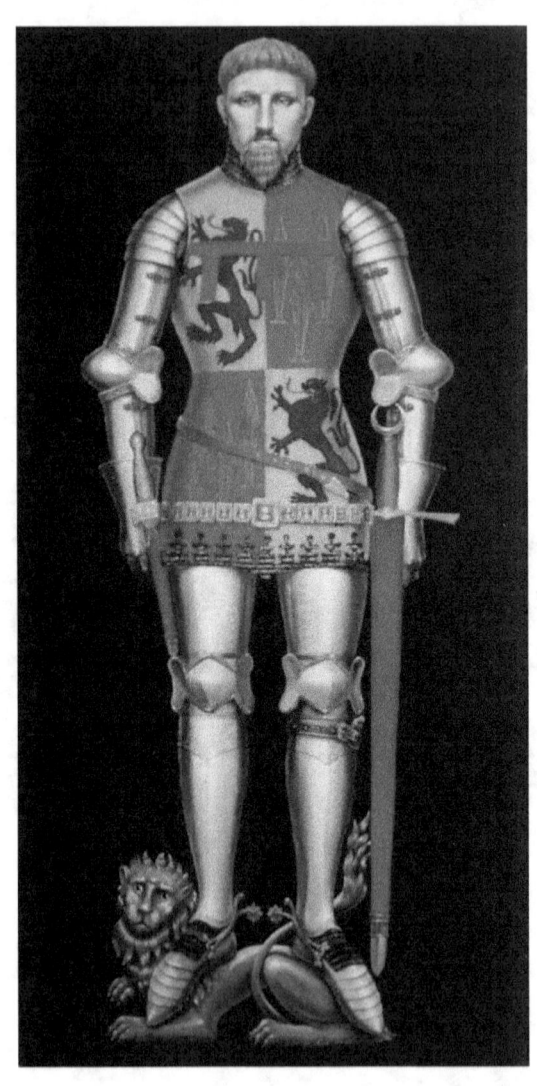

5. Harry Hotspur (The Inspiration Behind
Tottenham Hotspur's name)

110

6. John Ripsher (Founder of Tottenham Hotspur)

7. Charles Miller (British Founder of Brazillian
Football) – image source: Wikipedia

8. Paul Merson – image source: Wikipedia

9. Ricardo Kaká displaying his Christian
Faith

10. St. Domingo, Liverpool

Bibliography

INTRODUCTION

1. Peter Lupson – 'Thank God for FOOTBALL' Azure 2006

2. Richard Coles – 'Heart and Soul Faith and Football' 16.06.10 BBC World Service

3. James Walvin – 'The People's Game' Allen Lane 1975

FOREWORD

1. Richard Evans - 'The Factory Acts' Technical Education Matters 16.02.16.

2. 'St. George's Church, Everton 1814-1982' – The Church of St George, Everton in the county of Lancashire – ancashire online parish clerk project

3. Ian Sellars – 'Nonconformist attitudes in later nineteenth-century Liverpool' hslc.org.uk 15.03.1962

4. Op. Cit.

CHAPTER 1

1. C. Putney – 'Muscular Christianity' The encyclopedia of pedagogy and informal education http://www.infed.org/christianeducation/muscular_christian ity.htm 2003

2. Donald E. Hall – 'Muscular Christianity: Embodying the Victorian age' Cambridge University Press 2006

3. Brett and Kay McKay – 'Muscular Christianity – The Relationship between Men and Faith' Semper Virilis Publishing 2018

4. Dillon J Daine – 'How religious influence has Developed Sports into a Faith of its own' Bard College Spring 2020

5. John Simkin – 'The Encyclopedia of British Football Football and the Church' – spartacus-educational.com 1997

6. David Goldblatt – 'The Ball is Round a Global History of Football' Penguin

7. Skyler Jones – The push and pull of power: Organized Sports in Industrialized Britain' – Historical Studies 15 no. 60 1973

8. Op. Cit.

9. 'Industrialization, Labor, and Life – National Geographic society 11.11.24.

10. Eduard J Alvarez-Palau, Dan Bogart, Oliver Dunn, Max satchell + Leigh Shaw Taylor – 'Transport and Urban growth in the first industrial revolution' Cambridge Group for the History of Population 2020

11. 'The 1851 Religious Census' – Cambridge University Press 29.05.21.

12. Owen Chadwick – 'The Secularization of the European Mind in the 19th century' Cambridge 1975

13. Hugh McLeod – 'Religion and the people of Western Europe' 1789-1989 Oxford 1997

14. 'Science and Faith: The Industrial Revolution 9late 18th-19th Centuries) – rossway.net

15. Callum G Brown – 'The death of Christian Britain, Understanding Secularization 1800-2000' London 2001

16. Brett and Kay McKay – 'Muscular Christianity – The Relationship between Men and Faith' Semper Virilis Publishing 2018

17. Op. Cit.

18. Rebecca Alpert – 'American Muscular Catholicism: a brief history of catholic athletics in the United States, 1890-1950 Temple University 2022

19. David Tittterington – 'Muscular Christianity and the colonizing power of modern sports' Medium 15.05.2017

20. Brett and Kay McKay – 'Muscular Christianity – The Relationship between Men and Faith' Semper Virilis Publishing 2018

21. N.J. Watson, Stuart Weir + Stephen Friend – 'The development of Muscular Christianity in Victorian Britain and Beyond' Journal of Religion + Society Vol. 7 2005

22. Hugh Mcleod – 'The YMCA and the rise of modern sport' YMCA 175 History Papers April 2020

23. R. Holt – 'Sport and the British' Clarendon Press Oxford1989

24. Norman Vance – 'The Sinews of the Spirit: the ideal of Christian Manliness in Victorian Literature and Religious Thought' Cambridge University Press 1985

25. N.J. Watson, Stuart Weir + Stephen Friend – 'The development of Muscular Christianity in Victorian Britain and Beyond' Journal of Religion + Society Vol. 7 2005

26. C. Putney – 'Muscular Christianity' The encyclopedia of pedagogy and informal education http://www.infed.org/christianeducation/muscular_christianity.htm 2003

27. J.A. Mangan – '" Manufactured" Masculinity' Routledge 2013

28. John Simkin – 'The Encyclopedia of British Football and the Church' – spartacus-educational.com 1997

29. Donald E Hall – Muscular Christianity' Cambridge University Press 1994

30. David Goldblatt – 'The Ball is Round a Global History of Football' Penguin

31. Brett and Kate McKay – 'Muscular Christianity: Its History and lasting Effects' The Art of Manliness 16.07.19.

32. A. Parker + Nick J. Watson – 'Sport, Spirituality and Religion; Muscular Christianity and Beyond' Italian Review of the sociology of Religion' 2011

33. D.D. Molyneux – 'The development of physical recreation in the Birmingham district from 1871- 1892' MA thesis University of Birmingham 1957

34. Hugh Chisholm – 'Young Men's Christian Association' Encyclopedia Britannica Vol. 28 1911

35. Dominic Erdozain – 'The problem of pleasure' Woodbridge 2010

36. Michael Mazurkiewicz – 'Muscular Christianity: Christian Roots of American Sports' American History of Sports 2018

37. C. Putney – 'Muscular Christianity' The encyclopedia of pedagogy and informal education http://www.infed.org/christianeducation/muscular_christianity.htm 2003

38. James Walvin – 'The People's Game' Allen Lane 1975

39. Michael Mazurkiewicz – 'Muscular Christianity: Christian Roots of American Sports' American History of Sports 2018

40. Nicholas Watson – 'Muscular Christianity influenced the creation of the Modern Olympics' Christianity Today.com 08.02. 2018

CHAPTER 2

1. Hugh Mcleod – 'Religion and irreligion in Victorian England: how secular was the working class?' Bangor Headstart history 1993

2. E. R. Wickham – 'Church and People in an Industrial City' London 1957

3. Owen Chadwick – 'The Victorian Church Part One 1829-1859' London: Black 1966

4. Richard P. Heitzenrater – 'The poor and the people called Methodists' Abingdon Press 2002

5. AD Gilbert – 'Religion and Society in Industrial England 1740-1914' Longman 1976

6. Catherine Wessinger – 'The Oxford Handbook of Millennialism' Oxford University Press July 2016

7. Mark Burley – 'The history of sport in Public Schools' winchestercollege.org 18.05.20

8. Tony Collins – 'How Football Began a global history of how the world's football codes were born' Routledge 2019

9. Op. Cit.

10. Mark Burley – 'The history of sport in Public Schools' winchestercollege.org 18.05.20

11. Finn Ranson – 'The History of Football in Cambridge' Varsity 19.04.20.

12. Martin Johnes – 'A brief history of sport in the UK' in 'Encyclopedia of world sport' Berkshire Publishing 2005

13. Tony Collins – 'How Football Began a global history of how the world's football codes were born' Routledge 2019

14. Geoffrey Green – 'Soccer the World Game: A Popular History' Phoenix House 1953

15. David Goldblatt – 'The Ball is Round a Global History of Football' Penguin 2007

16. Tony Collins – 'How Football Began a global history of how the world's football codes were born' Routledge 2019

17. P. Swain – 'Early Football and the emergence of modern soccer: A reply to Tony Collins' The International Journal of the History of Sport 33 2016

18. Tony Collins – 'How Football Began a global history of how the world's football codes were born' Routledge 2019

19. Thomas John Preston – 'The origins and development of Association Football in the Liverpool District C.1879 until C.1915 University of Central Lancashire May 2007

20. David Goldblatt – 'The Ball is Round a Global History of Football' Penguin 2007

21. James Walvin – 'The People's Game' Allen Lane 1975

22. Rev'd Christopher Ramsay – 'Nineteenth century urbanisation and the Church of England, an assessment' Anglicanism.org 1995

23. Jonathan Este – 'How sport became the new religion – a 200-year story of society's 'great conversion' The Conversation 01.03.2023

24. Peter Lupson – 'Thank God for FOOTBALL' Azure 2006

25. A. Benkwitz – 'The emergence of and development of Association Football: influential sociocultural factors in Birmingham' 2017 University of Worcester

26. Tony Collins – 'How Football Began a global history of how the world's football codes were born' Routledge 2019

27. David Kessen – 'Sheffield home of football: Remarkable story of "world's first church football club"' The Star 17.05.24.

28. James Walvin – 'The People's Game' Allen Lane 1975

29. Jon Spurling – 'Highbury the story of Arsenal in N.5. London' 2007

30. 'Exeter Wesleyan United + Exeter Athletic' – The Grecian Archive

31. Peter Lupson – 'Thank God for FOOTBALL' Azure 2006

32. 'History' – bwfc.co.uk

33. Peter Lupson – 'Thank God for FOOTBALL' Azure 2006

34. Op. Cit.

35. Andrew Keenan – 'A Man's Game The birth of Mancunian football + the origins of Manchester City FC' CreateSpace 2013

36. Andrew Keenan – 'Are City a Protestant club?' – mancityhistory.com 22.11.23.

37. Bob Waterhouse – 'Everton: the fans Born not manufactured' Blue Horizon 2002

38. David Goldblatt – 'The Ball is Round a Global History of Football' Penguin 2007

39. Peter Lupson – 'Thank God for FOOTBALL' Azure 2006

40. D. Birley – 'Sport and the making of Britain' Manchester University Press 1993

41. A. Benkwitz – 'The Emergence and Development of Association f: influential sociocultural factors in Victorian Birmingham' 2017 University of Worcester

42. Richard Holt – 'Sport and the British: a modern history' Oxford University Press 1989

43. 'History of Birmingham City FC (1875-1965) wikiwand.com

44. Peter Lupson – 'Thank God for FOOTBALL' Azure 2006

45. 'The Beautiful history of club crests, Club Colours + Nicknames' - wordpress.com

46. Stewart, Steven Jamieson – Physical recreation and muscular Christianity in Glaswegian churches, 1865-1929' University of Glasgow 2021

47. Bob Waterhouse – 'Everton: the fans Born not manufactured' Blue Horizon 2002

48. Dr Anne Eyre – 'Football and relgious experience: sociological reflections'

49. 'The Brother Walfrid Story' – The Shamrock a celtic retrospective 06.04.15

50. Bill Murray – 'The Old Firm Sectarianism Sport and Society in Scotland' John Donald Publishers 1984

51. Scottish Sport – May 19th 1893

52. 'Club History' – Hibernian Community Foundation

53. 'Telegram Tam: Dundee Harp and the honest mistake' – The Shamrock a celtic retrospective' 12.01.19.

54. Rangers Fc a brief history' – therangersarchives.com

55. Bill Murray – 'The Old Firm Sectarianism Sport and Society in Scotland' John Donald Publishers 1984

56. Allan Laing – 'Ibrox lands double coup with Johnston' the Glasgow Herald 11.07.89.

57. The newsroom – 'The Old Firm story: how sectarianism came to define a derby' the Scotsman 01.07.16.

58. 'Use of Section 74 of the Criminal Justice (Scotland) Act 2003 – Religiously Aggravated Reported Crime: an 18-month review' Scotland.gov.uk. 18.12.16.

59. Hugh McLeod – 'How sport became the new religion – a 200-year story of society's "great conversion"' The Conversation 01.03.23.

60. 'The history of the Grand Old Team' – Belfast Celtic Society 11.02.09.

61. Owen Hargie, Ian Somerville and David Mitchell – 'Sport and peace in Northern Ireland' The association of Commonwealth Universities'

62. Stewart, Steven Jamieson – Physical recreation and muscular Christianity in Glaswegian churches, 1865-1929' University of Glasgow 2021

63. '10 things about St Johnstone' SPFL 26.11.14.

64. '10 things about St Mirren' SPFL 31.01.09.

65. Hugh Chisholm – 'Boys' Brigade' Encyclopedia Britannica Vol. 4 1911

66. John Springhall, Brian Fraser + Michael Hoare – 'Sure and Steadfast A History of the Boys' Brigade 1883-1983' Collins 1983

67. Stewart, Steven Jamieson – Physical recreation and muscular Christianity in Glaswegian churches, 1865-1929' University of Glasgow 2021

68. Peter Lupson – 'Thank God for FOOTBALL' Azure 2006

69. Op. Cit.

70. Martin Cloake and Alan Fisher – 'People's History of Tottenham Hotspur: how Spurs fans shaped the identity of one of the world's most famous clubs' Pitch Publishing 2016

71. Peter Lupson – 'Thank God for FOOTBALL' Azure 2006

72. Nicholas Spencer – 'Why Tottenham owe it all to a pauper' The Telegraph 24.09.07.

73. Peter Lupson – 'Thank God for FOOTBALL' Azure 2006

74. Op, Cit.

75. Victor Mather – 'Obscure club take stage as Champions League begins again' New York Times 29.06.15.

76. 'Chaplains keep faith in football' – Sports Chaplaincy UK 25.03.24.

77. Hugh McLeod – 'How sport became the new religion – a 200-year story of society's "great conversion"' The Conversation 01.03.23.

78. Richard Coles – 'Heart and Soul Faith and Football' 16.06.10 BBC World Service

79. Rob Sawyer – 'St Luke's – the church with its own football stadium' EFC Heritage Society 04.2021.

80. Joe Thomas – 'New Goodison Park role as Everton and St Luke's sow continued solidarity' Liverpool Echo 31.10.24.

81. 'Jesus given the red card' Sunday Life Belfast 11.06.14.

82. 'U19 Germany v U19 Belarus – Euro Qualifier' 11.10.11.

83. Andy Hunter – ' "People were telling us to go home": relegation and revival at Burnley' The Guardian 08.08.23.

84. The Newsroom – 'Ross County's religious chairman softens on Sunday Football' The Scotsman 13.03.16.

85. Catherine Priestley – 'Ex-Sunderland player and vicar united by faith and football' The Northern Echo 19.12.19.

86. 'Norfolk Christian Football league sees flocks flourish' BBC Norfolk 21.01.11.

87. Ben Russell – ' "Sporting, friendly and honest": The Manchester football league doing things differently' University of Central Lancashire 18.03.24

88. 'History' – Catholic United FC 13.07.19.

89. 'Faith + Football' – faithandfootball.org.uk

90. Mike Lockley – 'Football club with Christian links axed for 'singing Chelsea thugs' racist chant near black referee' The Mirror 11.03.15.

91. 'Maccabi GB Southern Football League' – Grassroots Football teamstats.net 30.06.24.

92. 'Belief in the game' – thefa.com

93. Adam Bate – 'Meet Punjabi Wolves, the fans' group bringing culture and noise to Molineux' The Guardian 15.12.15.

94. David Conn – 'Muslim youngsters' football club builds bridges and puts a smile on peoples' faces' The Guardian 01.06.16.

95. Gregory Ward + Chelle Gilham – 'Meet the female football team united in faith and football' euronews.com 12.12.22.

96. 'Faith in Football The campaign that ended FIFA's hijab ban' – Common Goal

97. NEWS WIRES – 'France's Senate backs bill to ban Muslim headscarf in sport competitions' france24.com 19.02.25.

98. Anbarasan Ethirajan – 'Facing Islamist threats, Bangladesh girls forced to cancel football matches' BBC News 18.02.25.

99. Samaya Farooq – "' Tough Talk", Muscular Islam and Football' in D. Burdsey – 'Race, Ethnicity and Football: Persisting Debates and Emergent Issues' Routledge 2011

CHAPTER 3

1. Tony Collins – 'Soccer: How the Global game became Global' Squarespace 25.04.16.

2. S. Alomes – 'Tales of a Dreamtime: Australian football as a Secular Religion' Australian Studies Nov. 01, 1993

3. Tony Collins – 'Soccer: How the Global game became Global' Squarespace 25.04.16.

4. Tony Collins – 'How Football Began a global history of how the world's football codes were born' Routledge 2019

5. Carlos Santacana + Manel Tomas – 'The origins of FC Barcelona's colours' fcbarcelona.com 27.12.16.

6. David Goldblatt – 'The Ball is Round a Global History of Football' Penguin 2007

7. Stuart + Philip Laycock – 'How Britain brought football to the world' The History Press 2022

8. David Goldblatt – 'The Ball is Round A Global History of Football' Penguin 2007

9. 'Banister's Court' – Sotonopedia wikidot.com

10. Aidan Hamilton – 'An entirely different game, the British influence on Brazilian football' Mainstream publishing 1998

11. David Goldblatt – 'The Ball is Round A Global History of Football' Penguin 2007

12. Juan Carlos Luziaga - 'Albion Football Club: profetas del sport en Uruguay' 05.08.

13. Op. Cit.

14. Stuart + Philip Laycock – 'How Britain brought football to the world' The History Press 2022

15. Op. Cit.

16. Ludwig Frieder – 'Football, Culture and Religion: Varieties of Interaction' Studies in World Christianity Vol. 21 Issue 3 Edinburgh University Press 2015

17. David Goldblatt – 'The Ball is Round a Global History of Football' Penguin 2007

18. Geoffrey James Levett – 'Playing the man: sport and imperialism 1900-1907

19. Daniele Serapiglia – 'Fe e futebol. Muscular Catholicism between Italy and Portugal in the European context (1922-1958) Sport el nationalismes 2019

20. David Goldblatt – 'The Ball is Round a Global History of Football' Penguin 2007

21. Ludwig Frieder – 'Football, Culture and Religion: Varieties of Interaction' Studies in World Christianity Vol. 21 Issue 3 Edinburgh University Press 2015

22. Stuart + Philip Laycock – 'How Britain brought football to the world' The History Press 2022

23. Tony Collins – 'How Football Began a global history of how the world's football codes were born' Routledge 2019

24. 'A turbulent founding on 19/12/1909' – BVB Club Website

25. Chris Lee – 'How football took off in Scandinavia' outsidewrite.co.uk 17.04.22.

26. Daniele Serapiglia – 'Fe e futebol. Muscular Catholicism between Italy and Portugal in the European context (1922-1958) Sport el nationalismes 2019

27. Stuart + Philip Laycock – 'How Britain brought football to the world' The History Press 2022

28. Op. Cit.

29. David Goldblatt – 'The Ball is Round A Global History of Football' Penguin 2007

30. Simon Engel – 'How Switzerland became a footballing nation' Swiss Sports History 06.04.23.

31. Jonathan Wilson – 'Angels with dirty faces' Orion 2016

32. Franklin Foer – 'How soccer explains the world: an unlikely theory of globalization' New York: Harper Collins 2004

33. Stuart + Philip Laycock – 'How Britain brought football to the world' The History Press 2022

34. Richard Holt - 'Sport and the British: A Modern History' Clarendon 1990

35. Brian Stoddart – 'Sport, "Cultural imperialism", and colonial response in the British Empire' Comparative Studies in Society and History' 30, no.4 1988

36. 'What was the role of sport in the British Empire?' – britishempire.me.uk

37. Joy Sports – 'The role of the church in Association Football' modernghana.com 06.04.19.

38. Afe Adogame, Nick J Watson + Andrew Parker – Global perspectives on Sports and Christianity' Routledge 2018

39. David Goldblatt – 'The Ball is Round a Global History of Football' Penguin 2007

40. Joy Sports – 'The role of the Church in Association Football' modernghana.com 06.04.19.

41. Stuart + Philip Laycock – 'How Britain brought football to the world' The History Press 2022

42. Op. Cit.

43. Op. Cit.

44. David Goldblatt – 'The Ball is Round a Global History of Football' Penguin 2007

45. P. Martin – 'Colonialism, Youth and Football in French Equatorial France' International Journal of the History of Sport,8,1, 1991

46. Afe Adogame, Nick J Watson + Andrew Parker – Global perspectives on Sports and Christianity' Routledge 2018

47. A. Odendaal – 'south Africa's Black Victorians: Sport and society in South Africa in the nineteenth century' I JA Mangan – 'Pleasure, profit, Proseltism: British Culture and Sport at Home and Abroad 1700-1814' London: Frank Cass 1988

48. Boria Majumdar and Kausik Bandyopadhyay – 'From recreation to Competition: early History of Indian football' A Social History of Indian Football: striving to score Routledge 2006

49. Abinand Lagisetti – ' "The Revenge of Plassey": Football in the British Raj' London School of Economics 20.07.20.

50. J.A. Mangan – 'How football came to Srinagar' The Kashmir Monitor 22.10.18.

51. Tony Mason – 'Football on the Maidan; Cultural Imperialism in Calcutta' The International Journal of the History of Sport 7 (1) 07.03.07

52. Dr. Mark Doidge – 'Football and Religion' Aga khan Centre

53. Brian Stoddart – 'Sport, "Cultural imperialism", and colonial response in the British Empire' Comparative Studies in Society and History' 30, no.4 1988

54. Abinand Lagisetti – ' "The Revenge of Plassey": Football in the British Raj' London School of Economics 20.07.20.

55. David Goldblatt – 'The Ball is Round a Global History of Football' Penguin 2007

56. Andrew Flint – 'A tale of one city: Kolkata' thefootballtimes.co 11.11.15.

57. Umaid Wasim – 'A football tournament in KP offers hope for the future' Dawn.com 16.12.24.

58. Sohail Shahrukh – 'Football: a league for Pakistan football' Dawn.com 28.04.24.

59. Stuart + Philip Laycock – 'How Britain brought football to the world' The History Press 2022

60. James Mills – 'Colonialism, Christians and Sport; the Catholic Church and football in Goa, 1883-1951' University of Strathclyde 2002

61. Op. Cit.

62. Stuart + Philip Laycock – 'How Britain brought football to the world' The History Press 2022

63. Ludwig Frieder – 'Football, Culture and Religion: Varieties of Interaction' Studies in World Christianity Vol. 21 Issue 3 Edinburgh University Press 2015

64. Stuart + Philip Laycock – 'How Britain brought football to the world' The History Press 2022

65. 'Maccabi Tel Aviv Official website' 30.08.15

66. 'Beitar Jerusalem, the most racist football club in Israel, gets an Arab owner' The Economist 10.12.20.

67. Paul Gittings – 'Israeli football club torched after signing Muslim players' CNN Sports 08.02.13.

68. 'Football thrives in Vatican City' – Inside FIFA 14.05.20.

69. Miguel Ciolczyck Garcia – 'Spain: Iconic chapel will return to Camp Nou' StadiumDB.com 09.02.25.

70. Ben Smith – 'World Cup 2014: Faith and football as Brazil unites to pray for glory' BBC Sport 08.07.14.

71. 'Kim Hyun-Hoi' – Nate 24.08.12.

72. Steve Vickers – 'Zimbabwe bans "religious" Amazulu' BBC Sport 05.11.05.

73. Abdo Gedeon – 'Mohammad Assi' 26.07.11.

74. Assile Toufaily – 'Football in Lebanon: a mirror of society?' Football makes History 24.05.24.

75. Barry Glendenning – 'Football teams for religion' 01.06.11. The Guardian

76. James M. Dorsey – 'Muslim Brotherhood takes to the soccer pitch' Alarabiya news 06.05.11.

77. Dr. Ewelina U Ochab – 'What does football have to do with religious freedom?' Forbes 08.07.18.

78. Salma Mousa - 'The impact of Inter-religious soccer leagues on social cohesion in post-ISIS Iraq' Innovations for Poverty Action 07.12.21.

79. Ronny Blaschke – 'Iran: where football meets religion' dw.com 20.06.18.

CHAPTER 4

1. Mike Huggins – 'The Victorians and Sport' Hambledon and London 2004

2. Peter Lupson – 'Thank God for FOOTBALL' Azure 2006

3. Op. Cit.

4. Jeffrey Cox – 'The English churches in a secular society Lambeth 1870-1930' Oxford University Press 1982

5. Hugh McLeod – 'How sport became the new religion – a 200-year story of society's "great conversion"' The Conversation 01.03.23.

6. Op. Cit.

7. A. Benkwitz – 'The Emergence and Development of Association f: influential sociocultural factors in Victorian Birmingham' 2017 University of Worcester

8. Tony Collins – 'How Football Began a global history of how the world's football codes were born' Routledge 2019

9. P. Bailey – 'Leisure and Class in Victorian England Rational Recreation and the contest for control 1830-1885' Routledge 2014

10. Hugh McLeod – 'How sport became the new religion – a 200-year story of society's "great conversion"' The Conversation 01.03.23.

11. Martin Johnes – 'Great Britain' in SW Pope, amp, John Nauright – 'Routledge Companion to Sports History' London 2010

12. Op. Cit.

13. Tony Collins – 'How Football Began a global history of how the world's football codes were born' Routledge 2019

14. 'The first professional footballer' – BBC Front Row

15.Tony Collins – 'How Football Began a global history of how the world's football codes were born'

16. Dave Russell – 'From evil to expedient: the legalisation of professionalism in English Football 1884-85' in Stephen Wagg – 'Myths and milestones in the history of sport' Palgrave 2011

17. DJ Taylor – 'On the Corinthian spirit' Yellow jersey press 2006

18. Tony Collins – 'How Football Began a global history of how the world's football codes were born' Routledge 2019

19. Johnathan Wilson – 'Sunderland's Victorian all-stars blazed trail for money's rule of football' The Guardian 25.04.20

20. 'Why football at Christmas is a very British tradition' BBC Bitesize

21. Mike Aitken – 'Scots passing pioneers shaped football' the Scotsman 06.03.11.

22. Tony Collins – 'How Football Began a global history of how the world's football codes were born' Routledge 2019

23. Op. Cit.

24. 'Attendance History' – Toffeeweb 2009

25. Bob Waterhouse – 'Everton the fans' Blue Horizon 2022

26. Joe Harston – 'Football's first genius (who kept pet foxes) - The Times 29.03.25.

27. 'Transfer System' – Spartacus International

28. Isaan Khan – 'The man who revolutionised football transfers: It's 60 years since George Eastham went on strike and changed the game forever' Daily Mail 04.07.23.

29. 'Who were the first British players to have been sold for record transfer fees?' – ITVX 15.07.23.

30. 'Transfers: spending on international deals hits record high of £7.6bn in 2023' BBC Sport 30.01.24.

31. 'Footballer wages' – Spartacus International

32. Paul W. – 'A short history of wages in English Football' The 1888 Letter 26.10.24.

33. Alex Miller + Nick Harris -'Revealed: Official English Football Wage Figures For The past 25 Years' – sportingintelligence.com 30.11.11.

34. 'How long does it take to match a footballer's weekly salary?' The HR Director 11.03.24.

35. Jason Stockwood – 'Time for a salary cap to keep leagues competitive and reduce agents' influence' The Guardian 15.02.24.

36. Philip Buckingham - 'PSR is not perfect, but the Premier League's shock therapy has had an effect' The Athletic 15.01.25.

37. Sam Green-Armytage – 'Premier League salary Cap – A governance perspective' Sp[orts Governance Academy 14.05.24.

38. John Harding – 'The Billy Meredith Story' Robson Books 1998

39. Peter Holland – 'Swifter than the Arrow: Wilfred Bartrop, Football and War' Troubador Publishing 2008

40. Andrew Ward + John Williams – 'Sixty years of the beautiful game' Bloomsbury 2009

41. Adam Volz – 'Bruce Grobelaar's Match-Fixing and bribery story explained' Casino.org 24.04,23.

42. Jim White – 'Bruce Grobelaar: match-fixing case was a dark time – players didn't know if I was a cheat' Daily Telegraph 07.02.25

43. 'FA betting rules' pitchero.com

44. K. Sankunni – '10 biggest betting scandals in football history' Sigma World 2025

45. 'UEFA had Forest-Anderlecht referee bribe evidence "for four years"' 25.09.16.

46. Dan Warren – 'Possibly the worst scandal of them all' BBC Sport 14.06.06.

47. J. Sugden + A. Tomlinson – 'Badfellas. FIFA family at war' Mainstream 2003

48. 'Boost for England's 2018 World Cup bid as FIFA want European host' Daily Mirror 19.02.10.

49. 'Bribery allegations over FIFA poll' – CNN 20/03/07

50. Owen Gibson – 'Joao Havelange resigns as FIFA honorary president over "bribes"' The Guardian 30.04.13.

51. James Montague – 'Corruption allegations rock Qatar's successful 2022 World Cup bid' CNN Sports 02.06.14.

52. David Oakley – 'Common ground? Sport and the church' The Bible Society Spring 2012

53. Hugh McLeod – 'How sport became the new religion – a 200-year story of society's "great conversion"' The Conversation 01.03.23.

54. 'The place where we worship the blues' – 'Goodbye to Goodison' - Liverpool Echo 2025

55. 'Residents raise concern with Linfield FC over Sunday games at Windsor Park' – Belfast Telegraph 08.08.22.

56. 'Sunday football: Northern Ireland Football League's proposal is rejected at Irish FA's AGM' BBC Sport 26.06.23.

57. 'IFA upholds Loughall's appeals over Sunday matches' BBC Sport 22.08.24.

58. Claire Cromie – 'Euro 2016: Northern Ireland to play first ever Sunday international at Windsor park' The Belfast Telegraph 16.03.16.

59. Tola Mbakwe – 'Pope: You can play sports on Sunday, if you still go to mass' Premier Christian News USA 05.06.18.

60. Neal Garnham – 'Association Football and society in pre-partition Ireland' Ulster Historical Foundation 2004

61. Firdose Moonda – 'African and Muslim' ESPN 30.05.14.

62. 'Iranian clerics demand national football team forfeit World Cup qualifier in case they celebrate goals during religious festival' The Independent 06.10.16.

63. Kyle Worley – 'Sports betting has become too prevalent for Christians to ignore' Christianity Today 19.09.24.

64. Hugh McLeod – 'The "Sportsman" and the "Muscular Christian" Rival ideals in nineteenth century England' Leuven University Press 2012

65. Pat McLoskey – 'Is gambling a sin?' Ask a Franciscan 14.05.20.

66. 'Gambling' – The Christian Institute

67. Mike Huggins – 'betting, Sport and the British, 1918-1939 Journal of Social History Vol. 41, no. 2, Winter 2007

68. 'Our football prize competitions' – Cricket and Football Field Bolton September 1887

69. W. Vamplew – 'Pay up and play the game. Professional sport in Britain, 1875-1914' Cambridge 1988

70. Stanley Rous – 'Football Worlds. A lifetime in sport' Faber + Faber 1978

71. Mark Clapson – 'A bit of a flutter. Popular gambling and British Society 1823-1961' History Today Vol. 41 issue 10 October 1991

72. Matthew Taylor – 'The Leaguers The making of Professional Football in England 1900-1939' Cambridge 2006

73. Piers Dudgeon – 'Our Liverpool memories of life in disappearing Britain' Hachette UK 2012

74. 'The history of betting on football' – Online Betting.ORG.UK

75. Christopher Jones – 'The development of the Football Pools in Britain during the Inter-War Years, 1918-1939, with particular reference to Littlewoods' Huddersfield University September 2018

76. Dave Russell – 'Football and the English. A social history of Association Football in England 1863-1995' Preston: Carnegie 1997

77. Christopher Jones – 'The development of the Football Pools in Britain during the Inter-War Years, 1918-1939, with particular reference to Littlewoods' Huddersfield University September 2018

78. Mark O'Haire – 'The History of Betting' The Set Pieces

79. Natalie Pirks + Tom Gundry – '29,000 gambling ads in Premier League weekend, says research' BBCSport 27.09.24.

80. 'The History of Football betting: from inceptions to Online Platforms' 12.06.24.

81. Alyssa Abrams – 'Guide to iGaming laws and Regulations throughout the world (2024) The Sumsuber 13.08.24.

82. Louise Taylor – 'Premier League clubs ban gambling sponsors on front of shirts from 2006-27' The Guardian 13.04.23.

83. Rob Davies – 'Regulator finds UK problem gambling rates may be eight times higher than thought' The guardian 23.11.23.

84. Brett Gibbons – 'Peter Shilton reveals 45-year gambling addiction hell as England legend speaks out' Birmingham Live 21.01.20.

85. Paul Merson – 'Hooked' Headline 2021

86. Bob Waterhouse – 'Everton the fans' Blue Horizon 2022

87. Andy Hunter – 'Everton sign betting sponsor deal two-years after terminating similar contract' The Guardian 09.06.22.

88. Faarea Masud + Ben King – 'Everton sponsor leaves UK after porn ad probe' BBC News 12.02.25.

89. Allison Lesley – 'FIFA aims to keep religion out of football' World Religion news 21.12.14.

90. Rob Harris – 'How rigid should football's rules be on expressions of religion?' Sky Sports 03.12.24.

91. Sportand Faithwriter – '10 Christian football players who are sharing their faith with the world' Sport faith 05.11.23.

92. Grace Holloway – 'Marc Guehi sparks controversy over Rainbow Laces campaign' roarnews.co.uk 14.12.24.

93. James Findlater – 'FA confirms Cody Gakpo decision as action taken after Liverpool star's celebration' Liverpool.Com 29.04.25

94. 'Ghana 1 Mali 0: Captain Wakaso faces ban for "Allah is Great" -shirt celebration' daily Mail 24.01.13

95. David Usborne – 'US soccer teams turn to religion to boost crowds' The Independent 04.06.06

96. Adam Shergold – '£5m a year to be NICE! Committed Christian Neymar "has an ethical clause in his PSG contract agreeing to avoid political or religious controversy, be

courteous and punctual and meet the fans"' Daily Mail 14.09.21.

97. 'Did Christian star soccer player Jaelene Hinkle miss out on the World Cup because she was kicked off the team by "virtue-signaling feminists" after refusing to wear a Gay Pride jersey in 2018 because it went against her beliefs?' Daily Mail 11.07.18.

98. Nicolas Vilas – 'Dieu Football Club' Hugo Sport 2014

99. Etienne Ferie – 'Witness This I'm a former top footballer who was compared to George Best but I quit at 23 to become a Jehovah's Witness' The Sun 13.09.23

100. Aimee Lewis –'When football's final whistle blows' BBC Sport 19.03.08

101. Tom Dart – 'Gavin Peacock departs for religious journey' The Times 06.09.08.

102. Mariecke van den Berg – 'More openly religious football players in the Orange football team' Vrije University Amsterdam 24.06.24.

103. Sam Matthews Boehmer – 'The unstoppable rise of Christianity in football' The Spectator 12.01.25.

104. Julian Coman – 'God-given talent: Saka, Rashford and Sterling blaze a trail for black British Christians' The Observer 17.07.21

105. Jenkins – 'Marcus Rashford is keeping Christianity in the British limelight' The Christian Century 12.01.22.

106. Gary Jacob – 'how £15m buy became Palace cult hero' The Times 29.03.25.

107. John Maiden – 'Football, lived religion and public piety' The Open University 23.07.21.

108. Firdose Moonda – 'African and Muslim' ESPN 30.05.14.

109.   Phil Minshull – 'Devout worshipper' BBC Sport 12.12.07.

110.   Ian Williams – 'Faith comes before football' BBC Sport Africa 24.03.25

111.   Pete Brooks – 'Real Madrid make small but deliberate change to their crest for UAE island partnership' Sports.Yahoo.com 30.03.12.

112.   Dr. James Dorsey – 'Saudi soccer: A game of geopolitics and religion, not just sports' Modern Diplomacy 06.08.23.

113.   Hugh McLeod – 'How sport became the new religion – a 200-year story of society's "great conversion"' The Conversation 01.03.23.

114.   'Purpose,   Vision,   Mission'   – evertoninthecommunity.org

115.   'Who We Are' – evertoninthecommunity.org

116.   Henry Winter – 'Everton are a shining beacon as a force for good in the community' 10.01.15 Daily Telegraph

117.   'The Premier League's investment in numbers' premierleague.com 21.04.24.

118.   Marco Carlotti – 'The social value of the Premier League: clubs and local communities at the core' 16.01.25.

119.   'How are Premier League clubs helping the local community during pandemic?' allfootballapp.com 24.03.20.

120.   Gerald Gallagher – 'Faith: in search of the greater glory of sport' Hero Books 2022

121.   Jack Stanley – 'How a professional football player manages fasting during ramadan' mrporter.com 22.03.23.

122.   Latifa Babas – 'European football leagues adapt to Ramadan: Breaks for fasting players gain momentum' en.yabiladi.com 03.03.25

123.   'Arnaut Danjuma: Football and Faith' versus.uk.com 20.03.23.

124.   'Islam in football. The profound effect the religion has on the game' Hubpages 10.04.20.

125.   Tusdiq Din – 'Premier League clubs are making progress over prayer rooms for fans' The Guardian 10.09.15.

126.   Ben Smith – 'World Cup 2014: Faith and football as Brazil unites to pray for glory' BBC Sport 08.07.14.

127.   Hanna Tervanotko – 'Analysis: Soccer and religion have more in common than you might think' Mcmaster University 19.07.24.

128.   Richard Coles – 'Heart and Soul Faith and Football' 16.06.10 BBC World Service

129.   Ben Bird – 'how Mohamed Salah inspired me to become a Muslim' The Guardian 03.10.19.

CHAPTER 5

1. Owen Chadwick – 'The Victorian Clergy' London 1970

2. Thomas John Preston – 'The origins and development of Association Football in the Liverpool District C.1879 until C.1915 University of Central Lancashire May 2007

3. 'Liverpool' – A Dictionary of Methodism in Britain and Ireland'

4. Hugh Chisholm – 'Methodist New Connexion' - Encyclopedia Britannica 1911

5. 'Aug 30 The Rev Chambers, Everton + Liverpool' – The pearl of Great Price podcast 30.08.21.

6. Bob Waterhouse – 'Everton the fans' Blue Horizon 2022

7. Thomas John Preston – 'The origins and development of Association Football in the Liverpool District C.1879 until C.1915 University of Central Lancashire May 2007

8. Op. Cit.

9. Thomas Keates – 'History of the Everton Football Club 1878-1928' Desert Island Football Histories 1928

10. Mike Royden – 'Thomas Keates – Director and First Historian of Everton Football Club' Everton FC Heritage Society 09.09.23.

11. Thomas John Preston – 'The origins and development of Association Football in the Liverpool District C.1879 until C.1915 University of Central Lancashire May 2007

12. David Starsky – 'St Domingo's and the birth of Everton Football Club' (talk by Peter Lupson) The Everton Collection Talks 20.10.09.

13. Thomas Keates – 'History of the Everton Football Club 1878-1928' Desert Island Football Histories 1928

14. Floreat Evertonae – 'History of the Everton Football Club' 1893 (in The David France Collection)

15. Thomas Keates – 'History of the Everton Football Club 1878-1928' Desert Island Football Histories 1928

16. Norman F Swain – 'A short history of St. Domingo Methodist Church Everton Liverpool 1871-1971

17. Mike Royden - Everton Village + the Birth of Everton Football Club' 13.12.24.

18. Thomas John Preston – 'The origins and development of Association Football in the Liverpool District C.1879 until C.1915 University of Central Lancashire May 2007

19. Peter Lupson – 'The Holy Trinity of Our Forefatherspart111: Dr James Clement Baxter' 23.01.17. Everton FC Heritage Society

20. 'George Mahon (1853-1908)' – merseysidebiographies.weebly.com

21. David Kennedy + Michael Collins – 'Community Politics in Liverpool and the Governance of Professional Football in the Late Nineteenth Century' – The Historical Journal 49,3 2006

22. Thomas Keates – 'History of the Everton Football Club 1878-1928' Desert Island Football Histories 1928

23. David Kennedy + Michael Collins – 'Community Politics in Liverpool and the Governance of Professional Football in the Late Nineteenth Century' – The Historical Journal 49,3 2006

24. Op. Cit.

CONCLUSION

1. Hugh McLeod – 'How sport became the new religion – a 200-year story of society's "great conversion"' The Conversation 01.03.23.

2. Joseph 1832 – 'Football, a religion that unites like no other' Nairaland Forum 22.11.12.

www.ingramcontent.com/pod-product-compliance
Lightning Source LLC
Chambersburg PA
CBHW071755120626
46550CB00002B/803